Q

BOP

CITY

Q

BOP

CITY

VINCENT QUATROCHE

To order additional copies of this book, contact:
Xlibris
1-888-795-4274
www.Xlibris.com
Orders@Xlibris.com
780788

CONTENTS

Acknowledgements

Cover Art

Sutton Place

Vincent Quatroche Sr.

Circa mid 1950s

Previous Works

Print
Another Rubber Eden 1997
Attitude House 2002
Greetings from Gridville 2006
CyberStein 2007
The Terrible Now 2009
21 Short Dog Stories 2011
(Collected Short Fiction)

Sometimes Grief- *barks up the wrong tree* 2012

Got Abstract? 2014

*

Audio
Matador from Another Planet 2002
In Dreamthink 2006
Vanishing Breed 2008
(Collected 90s cassette series recordings Vol 1)

Singing Mr. Cedric 2010

Quattro-Vox 2013
Seeing Eye Ear 2017 Digital edition/Revised CD format 2018
For more information regarding the availability these works
Please visit www.rubbereden.com

Here we are, trapped in the amber of the moment. There is no why."
-Kurt Vonnegut

"It has been said, 'time heals all wounds.' I do not agree. The wounds remain. In time, the mind, protecting its sanity, covers them with scar tissue and the pain lessens. But it is never gone."
-Rose Kennedy

"There's never enough time to do all the nothing you want."
- Bill Watterson

Sarcasm is the weakest weapon
- Reid Mahaffy Sr.

The poet is, etymologically, the maker. Like all makers, he requires a stock of raw materials — in his case, experience. Now experience is not a matter of having actually swum the Hellespont, or danced with the dervishes, or slept in a doss-house. It is a matter of sensibility and intuition, of seeing and hearing the significant things, of paying attention at the right moments, of understanding and co-coordinating. Experience is not what happens to a man; it is what a man does with what happens to him. It is a gift for dealing with the accidents of existence, not the accidents themselves. By a happy dispensation of nature, the poet generally possesses the gift of experience in conjunction with that of expression.
-Huxley, Aldous. *Texts and Pretexts.*

"There's a place beyond words where experience first occurs to which I always want to return. I suspect that whenever I articulate my thoughts or translate my impulses into words, I am betraying the real thoughts and impulses which remain hidden."
-Jerzy Kosiński, The Painted Bird

Somebody asked me: "What do you do? How do you write, create?" You don't, I told them. You don't try. That's very important: not to try, either for a Cadillac, creation or immortality. You wait, and if nothing happens, you wait some more. It's like a bug high on the wall. You wait for it to come to you. When it gets close enough you reach out, slap out and kill it. Or if you like it's looks, you make a pet out of it."
- Charles Bukowski

Foreword

Q Bop City is collection of recent written work produced since the 2014 publication of ***Got Abstract?*** Included are selections from some very important people and experiences that have helped shape perspective and voice that composes both the POV and sensibilities of my expression, I recently ran across a collection of Poetry written by my father Vincent Quatroche Sr. in a yellowed with age Manuscript (never published) from the late 1940s written very soon after he mustered out of the Air Force at the conclusion of WW 2. While he was recognized primarily for his artist talents, the poems included provide a rare intimate glimpse of a very young man's passion and love for life. As I have always contended my father was my first teacher who had a seminal influence on my perception of what constituted creative expression later in life.

Of significance as well is the inclusion of selected poems and translations from my old friend, colleague and mentor Professor Emeritus David Lunde who taught Creative Writing for many years in the English Department at SUNY Fredonia NY. It was his initial support and encouragement that was essential to my decision to publish my first collection of Poetry and Prose in 1998 **Another Rubber Eden.** I would acknowledge his influence and presence in my creative life as important as my father's role. I regarded him as one of my brothers in life.

The collection of perspectives entitled A **Life Sentence-A Day at a Time** are reflections of teaching in the Chautauqua County Jail in Mayville NY over the course of fourteen years as an GED adult educator appear in this effort as well. Previously published in my books over the years this is their first appearance as a single body of work. The time I did in that capacity was a life changing experience that provided a unique insight and perspective into the lives of those incarcerated and the men and women who labored as correction officers in a legal system that few outside the bars ever experience or have some understanding of that reality.

There is also included some work from and about a few NYC poets, who over the years have become close friends and confidants. There is always the popular perception that Poetry doesn't pay and the value of the endeavor limited at best. Well- perhaps that might be valid on a very superficial level however I have been made rich beyond words with gift of these eclectic souls friendship and support in readings in NYC that I have participated in and generously been included in that community.

As a general assessment of my work included here I have no glib appraisal. Perhaps I do write a kind of Rescue Dog Poetry after all. There are new pieces-some lost and found revisions and of course the usual fragments, shorts, non sequitur mutts that escaped the animal shelter of obscurity. A curious section entitled Cyber-Funnies lost and found in the Spam attempts to give the reader some inkling of the strange cryptic cyber world that my website Rubber Eden has attached over the years. They are presented in the spirit of Stan Mack who used to write in the old Village Voice. Anonymously submitted the reactions, the comments and at times humorous in a very nasty sort of way I began to collect and even display the cryptic remarks on the Rubber Eden Website in a section entitled lost & found in the Spam. Actually I probably never would have been aware of their existence if not for the analytics plug-in on the Word Press hosting site. Once I started to check the folder years ago I was increasing impressed by the acrimony and venom forwarded/directed in my direction. Of course the question remains were they specifically addressing me personally? That I don't know or even really care. But I will say this much- they are the flower of the BS that goes on in the Cyber World.

Speaking of which I still firmly resist participating in any of the myriad of Social Media platforms that have flourished and multiplied in the last ten years. I regard sites like Facebook a middle aged skin disease like Shingles. Even my own little cyber vanity mirror Rubbereden devoted to underground expression in writing, the arts, film, music and creative abstraction has long since lost its charm or importance in my life. I usually update once a month and even that exercise has become at times either a chore or a bore. It could vanish tomorrow (and just might someday if I decide to pull the plug on it) and really it wouldn't be a great loss I think.

What you are reading and holding in your hands perhaps in book format now has become dinosaur like anachronism relegated to that small plastic device that that the culture (sic) is addicted to and can't seem to get their nose out of for two seconds. Just remember this hair trigger fragile Grid we all worship could disappear overnight too. And I'm afraid it just might and then my friend it will all be a brave new world in the Terrible Now.

Not too long ago I was having a conversation with an old friend of forty plus years (who actually has read my work) at Meyers Bar and he remarked that nobody really wanted to hear about my insecurities, fears, failures and personal end game babble. He said yeah you're pretty good sometimes, but you should write about *happy stuff.* Adding he was only telling me this as a friend. So how come every time somebody prefaces an observation of this nature it's always something vaguely unpleasant and judgmental, seldom *happy stuff.* Regardless to a degree I understand his advice and I get his point. Truth be known? He's probably a much better mechanic than I'm a writer. But we both in our own ways try to make stuff run. So as our old friend Bo Boone used to say- *Do you see it? You don't see it. See it there.*

Vincent Quatroche July 2018

Where is Lucky Ward?

Where is lucky Ward tonight...is he out of cigarettes
or don't he need them anymore?
Is Hot Horse calling him up and in his best three
day drunk voice asking,
"Well, Hiya you old bastard, Why aren't you dead yet?
And if you were... how would you ever tell?"
"Dammit," he goes "...my phone don't ring for a week,
then I get three phone calls in an hour...two
wrong numbers and this.... I just don't see the
difference."
All the rest of you smart ass bastards have got
machines to screen things out...Now I'll ask you what
have I got?"
The line went silent.
"Smatter, out of questions?"
Hot Horse could feel Lucky's grin in the receiver.
"Want news don't you...the details....divorce...infidelity
Drunken confessions..alibi's ....bragging either how much
money I make or how much I owe...Well you can forget it."

The silence went on longer this time.
"Yikes," thought Hot Horse, "I only wanted to ask
how his kid's were."

Then Lucky Ward said, "Keep away from me, there pal;
Don't know you anymore. Just too long ago to be bothered
digging up a bunch of old bones for a little leftover meat."
"Yeah, I remember you. So what. How'd you get this number
anyway, it's unlisted." Oh," Hot Horse "ran into an old friend of
yours."
"Yeah, like who?" Now Lucky Ward is interested.

The silence went on and on and then clicked,
like the sound of old plastic faceplate's switch,
or gravel and dirt falling off a shovel followed by the dial
tone.

Now in the bar, it's Hot Horse who has the grin.
He whispering, *"Love that man."*

2/91

Beat Poetry Horse Race

Well hello there beat poetry race fans
Welcome to the 5th race at Bukowski Downs
It's been raining cats & dogs & angel headed hipsters since dawn
And the track is sloppy.
There at the post
There's the bell

And there off!

Cryptic stranger is strong off the line
With sentimental tripe on his heels
Followed by Pretentious Prose
Rounding out the top three.
While Cosmic Babble
Humorless Despair and Bargain Basement Bathos
are in hot pursuit in the second tier.

In the middle of pack
Grey beard confusion
Suicide Blond
Ethnic disaster
And Gender Axe to Grind

Bringing up the rear
Iambic Pentameter Masturbator
Drunken Rant
&
Colon Cacophony

Around the 1st turn

Cryptic Stranger is holding by 2 lengths

Pretentious Prose & Sentimental Tripe
Are neck and neck
Gary Beard confusion wants the outside lane
While Suicide Blonde is deciding if she wants
To fuck him after the race.
Humorless Despair is dropping back
Cosmic Babble seems confused
Bargain Basement Bathos has started to weep.
Gender Axe to Grind & Ethnic Disaster
Trade places and vendettas
At the halfway point now

The pack is starting to spread

Cryptic Stranger still holding his own
Pretentious Prose & Sentimental Tripe
Are losing focus and fading out of the top three
While Cosmic Babble seems poised to make a move

Iambic Pentameter Masturbator beats it
Drunken Rant has gone to the whip
& Colon Cacophony refuses to quit.

On the last turn now
Headed towards the finish line

Cryptic Stranger has opened up a lead to four lengths
Cosmic Babble has a lane on the outside
Humorless Despair now slips into the 3 spot

And here comes Colon Cacophony out of nowhere

Down to the Wire Now

And it's the Cryptic Stranger running out of gas
With Cosmic Babble on his heels
Coming on strong Humorless Despair

This going down to the wire
Going to be a photo finish

And it's Colon Cacophony by an Anus!

Please hold all tickets
Till the official results have been posted on the
Track Tote Board by a literary agent.

The 18th Sunday of Ordinary Time

After going to St. Agnes for early morning mass that Sunday with Edna
We stopped at the IGA and I happened to run across by chance one of
My poems in the frozen food isle.

It was about 70 years now and had on a pink pin striped shirt w/
   button down
Collars and gold wire rim glasses sporting a dignified full head of
   neatly cropped
Snow white hair that when it spotted me out of the blue years
   exclaimed in pure
Wonderment as I crossed his path near the potato chips

My God......are you still alive?

The nature of the observation was delivered in anything far from a
Congratulatory intonation or tone.

Stunned I merely shrugged and went out to the car to put away the
   groceries
In the back seat and tell my mom I forgot something inside the store and
Would be right back.

Marched right into the IGA again. Quickly scanning all the isles for the
Son of a bitch. Spotted him in the canned vegetables next to the
   Succotash.
Ran that Poem down- and he saw me coming and was none too happy
   about it.

I confronted it and introduced myself and forced it to shake my hand and
Asked just what the hell as the meaning of pervious remark?

At this point it got real sheepish, with lower eyes mumbling something

About Lucky Ward and hastily shoved off to meat counter.

And I couldn't resist I yelled after him-

Yeah well- you always were a lousy poem anyway

4/16/2016

10/10/10

There is this perfume
arresting these moving objects
were the chill is gently roaring
away high in the tree tops
you can see your place
in all this slipping
your grasp on your flesh declining
a liquid moment flowing
the weight of time insisting
draining you away from all
you ever knew of yourself
in this tenuous truce
with the tactile world reality
You are being pulled
out further in the Sound from the shore
A matter of dissolution in salt time
A shadow tide reoccurring
seasons removing you
barely buoyant now
upon diminishing reasons
to hold on to a deflating floatation device
Yours orange dreams limp
losing shape
just enough vision and sound left
to clearly realize
all that is beyond your reach
All that you struggle to remember
barely recalling now
the fleeting touch
the scent of a distant fleeting perfume
lingering about the concussion

of dried leaves striking the blacktop
Your very dry land and its anchor
left above the waterline
buried in the beach.

10/10

V.I.A.I

Very Important Abstract Information

The only 16 letter word that can be spelled without repeating a letter
    is *uncopyrightable*
The average person laughs thirteen times a day
In Tennessee it's against the law to drive a car while sleeping
While in Kentucky, it's a law that a person must take a bath once a year
Alaskan law says you cannot look at a moose from an airplane
In the 13th Century Europeans baptized children with beer
Benjamin Franklin gave guitar lessons
The electric chair was invented by a Dentist
A person sneezing was the first thing Thomas Edison filmed with
    his movie camera
If you refrigerate your rubber bands- they will last longer
Pound of pound hamburgers cost more that new cars
Americans eat 12 Billion Bananas a year
A Crocodile cannot stick its tongue out
Some lions mate 50 times a day
Butterflies taste with their feet
When you look at someone you love-your pupils dilate- and they do
exactly the same when you are looking at someone you hate.
Not only do Ants sleep they stretch when they wake up in the morning
The average dream lasts 2 to 3 seconds

6/2018

Meet the Ancient Mariner (for PG)

I sat down before a poetry reading over on 15th Street at the Revival
    Bar last Summer
On a stool open between us- at first glance out of the corner of my eye
He struck me as a classic tough ass old New Yorker chewing gum that
Would gladly deck/knock the block off of the nearest wise guy punk
Who would ask for it by running his yap barking up the wrong tree or
Perhaps it might be just a look in his general direction he didn't like.

Now this guy was in shape to boot with dignified duds, closely
cropped white hair and impeccably groomed mustache smoothly
    nursing a drink with a folder in front of him on the bar.
I was thinking Union Boss, Mob Goodfella or Teamster Rep. chilling
    after work

So the seat I'm planted in between us there is this GD air conditioner
    unit blowing
Ice cubes down my neck and I want to move over the bar stool open
    between us
(All the other spots were taken)

So I decide to make the move and keep my pie hole buttoned up as
    to why
Even if he decides that I'm some friggin fruit trying to make a move.

Bartender goes – *guess that seat got to you too*
Little too cool there huh boss?

Which adding a reaction my man says- *yeah I was there at first*
When I came in- had to make a move over here.

Chewing that gum he's sizing me up.
With this beatific spark in his eye.

VINCENT QUATROCHE

I slug my beer down and head up the stairs to the reading.
In few minutes The Ancient Marnier shows up.

Shrugging at me in recognition of some sort that suggests he has
Figured out you're another poet as well.

He was thinking downstairs much the same about you before at the
    bar before
Contractor or hardass something or other.

And since then we discovered we were brothers from another mother.

8/7/2015

Steam Heat Cool

Hottest day of the Summer so far that year
In mid July on fricasseeing 1ˢᵗ Ave and as I'm
Doing a steady sweaty schlep approaching
The corner of 12ᵗʰ street
And this eighty year old guy appears
in the heat waves like an oasis mirage
In a powder blue double breasted suit jacket with
Boxed square cut shoulders like Cab Callaway used to sport,
His cream dress shirt with ruffled button down trim has a mile
Wide grape tinted tie freshly off the rack from the 40s held
perfectly centered with a gleaming diamond stick pin clasp
tan trousers with crisp razor creases, heeling toeing spotless
white bucks with pink shoes topped off with an extra wide brimmed
vanilla fudge swirl Fedora and Harlequin blue sunglasses
And not a drop
And man I mean not drop
Of sweat on him.

July 16

Your Second Skin

Deep in your second skin
The protoplasm brain
Provides this epidermal mind
Nervous system undercurrents
That are always flowing
In your memory voice
Without filter, restraint or abatement.

There will be no controlling
The tidal wave of self-message
It crackles, erupts
Haunts and persists
No mercy deep in this second skin
Respite or alibi.

Clearly we are not
Of this world
Our past trails behind us
As a rickety platform
Form the Terrible Now.

So what just the drives this future?
That second skin you just
Stepped upon
In a heel toe goose stepping march.

We are so murdered
On a daily basis.

Come Back Big Mike

For Big Mike

Where have you gone Big Mike?
We missed being yelled at by you
We need to be yelled at by you.
Please come back and bellow at us-
Shake your fist in our faces
And if we don't like it?
Offer to kick our ass for us.

We deserve it certainly
Been asking for it.
Yeah- We have it coming.
Bring back that booming voice
Step up to the box in the front of the room
Swing from the heels with your linguistic Louisville slugger
40 ounce baseball bat indignation
Squaring one up.

Just stand up there and reread the riot act of anything that
Pops up in your head that's driving you crazy.

Chances are?
It's driving us crazy too.

It's been too quiet. It's been too long
Since anybody around here had the guts
To let fly without restraint or remorse
Your gift for volatile exasperated rage…

So please come back Big Mike
Smack us around like in the old days
Pin our ears back take us down a peg
Teaching us all a lesson
We won't forget in a hurry.

6/17

The End of the Semester Faculty Party

So it's a beautiful mid afternoon June day.
I'm trying to fight off this hangover
And work on this manuscript for yet another collection
Of suspect Po and Prose that nobody really wants anyway
As evidenced by last eight books that never really sold and were
    widely ignored.

I thinking about the end of the semester faculty party that my chair
Reminded me about yesterday and wanted to know if I was planning
    to attend.
Honestly I had forgotten about it and would have been more that
    content
To skip the entire scene and just be MIA staying home drinking beer and
Try to convince myself I need to work on this project.

But now I've talked myself into it seeing as it is a going away party for
A couple of colleagues- one is retiring and the other is jumping ship for
More dough down in Jersey.

The former it took years to get to know and be friendly with.
Near the end we kind of connected over a mutual student who
Was a super bright menacing time bomb who was generally annoying
And scaring the shit out of both students and other professors in the
    Department.
As I recall the College student affairs had identified him as a
Student of concern referring him to counseling Center.

Now I wish her nothing but the best.
Should really tell her that and say goodbye.

In general I like my colleagues, we usually get along ok
And the host of the affair is a good friend mine anyway.

As for the latter-
The smarmy bastard over the years hasn't even tried to hide his
    disdain for me.
In more than one interminable faculty meeting seldom missed an
    opportunity
To express his disrespect towards me either in snide comment or
    disgusted facial
Expression whenever I spoke up about something.

So tonight I've got to really watch myself
Keep track of the beers
And resist the very real impulse if I sense him giving me any shit
Of walking over to him and bitch slap his silly skinny stupid ass
Knocking that smirk off to the other side of his face.

So I'm going to ride my bike after I finish writing this
Out to the park near the lake- cool off and giving myself
A good talking to about he's not worth the trouble
And ruin the party for everybody else settling so trivial
Hash with this dickhead who's headed down the road anyway.

When I get home after the ride
Just take a long shower
Get dressed and get ready to
Be picked up by my Chair and his wife
And make nice.

So when we get there
I set up my lawn chair and cooler of beer on ice
That just happens to be next to dickhead's wife.
She immediately moves down to the other end of the Patio.

I lean forward and shoot her a long purpose pitch look
Thinking- *that's ok baby I know what you're expecting me to act like.*
But I took care of that in the shower before I got here.

6/18

The Colleagues Talk 2.0

Kafka on Kampus (for K)

As he was pulling out the parking slot on a sweltering Thursday noon
His colleague came running up flagging him down waving his arms
With this wild look in his eyes and breathlessly exclaimed
The administration has sold the naming rights to the college!

He immediately pulled back in and cut the motor
Got out and stood before him and replied- *say what?*

Catching his wind gasped *that's right- the bastards just posted the news*
On Prof talk- it's official starting this Fall Semester this school is
Now named Kafka Kollege –a yes that's Kollege w/ a GD K

No Shit he remarked *are you kidding me?*

His colleague shook his head emphatically and continued......

And that's not the half of it- all of the buildings on Kampus have been
    renamed
As well as part of the agreement-
All the Dorms are now called The Penal Colony
The Kampus Center is The Castle
The Theater Department is The Hunger Artist
Academic Affairs? The Judgment
English? Parables & Paradoxes
Science? The Metamorphosis
Public Safety?-Before the Law
Human Resources? The Trial
Student Affairs? Give it up

We stood in stunned silence sweating in the oppressive summer heat
Then my colleague broke into this really strange serine smile
And purred out-
But I do have some rather good news-
Seems all the Administrators, Deans & Chairs even the President
Have been transformed into Ungeheuer Ungeziefers (literally
        "monstrous vermin")
like Cockroaches and Dung Beetles
and are hiding in their offices under the desks.

8/2017

Education

For Sarah

They were the Teachers
They were the Vehicles

The blunt object
That forced their door open
Just a crack so could think escape.

They were the spark
The enablers.
Telling you on a fog shrouded
Far away beach one afternoon this-

That everything was only not permitted
Forbidden and questionable-
But possible.

So I let you
And you let me
So much that followed
Was a dream that
Came true
To some degree.

Some pay up front
For all to see
A reason
A curse
Rendered ransom relegated to some stray verse

Some pay up front
For all to see
In the face of what we once
aspired to be.

5/26/17

Crossword Poetry

For Darren

Down

1. Robert Mitchum in the Kitchen's Film Noir gear shift
3. Those who listen around Corners hear
5. Greek Painter who laughed himself to death
7. Beer makes you smart drinking is
9. Sam Cooke and The Pretenders are working on

Across

1. Bowie fell here looking for
4. Eno's finks don't do this
6. Lincoln had no laughs here
8. Mr. Ed's wires did this
10. PT 109 Borgnine
12. Stairway to Smith Haven Mall lead singer
14. Beckett's Laurel & Hardy are waiting for

Down

11. Nobody Walks in LA
13. Being Fail Safe Dr. Strange Love there
15. Picnic basket Catcher
17. Beat respite between Dunkin Ds and Mickey Bs
19. Big Mountain E9th long ago between 1 & 2nd Ave.
21. Rolling Stone Preferred Pigment

Sound Light

And then the sun went
Behind the clouds
Mid-afternoon on a
Mild late September Sunday.

McCoy Tyner played
West Philly Tone Poem
On the radio.

Somewhere in the next yard
Over
A crow had a good hard
Laugh.

The colors in here are trying
To embrace me.
Console and soften
A hard edged truth
About loss and remorse.

As a freight high balled
At the grade on the mainline
Next block over
While the engineer
This time didn't hit the horn
Three times as he usually did
But I distinctly heard
A voice say
Your time is coming.

10/11

Swinging for the Fences in Q-Bop City

Of Odds & Pitch Counts

Some people are born
With two strikes on them
Others start out with the count 3 and 0
And go through life
Always content to just take that walk
While the former keep swinging at that one in the dirt.

If Only

If you could only
just write one poem
that sounded like
Ben Webster's
Tenor Saxophone
Then maybe
somebody might
listen to you.

I bet infinity

is just endless talk
or worse yet....

Discuss.

Burning June

Each June sunset
burns like a stick match
struck against balance
left in the calendar box.

Right now I've got 27 left.
But who's counting?
I am.

How the West was Lost

Have we all become a race
Of distracted cyber pioneers
Too embarrassed to admit
All that we never knew is
the only remarkable thing about us
Remembering the trivial
Forgetting the essential.

*

Hearing Aide

Received a postcard in the mail yesterday
Offering either an agnostic apostle
Or generic prosthesis-

And I didn't hear a thing.

*

Fuck Waste book

Listen here
You can just skip the Like Box
And the dislike Box
Heading straight for the
I don't give a shit Box.

Trio Striking Attitudes in Rome

Overheard on Train 284 from Buffalo to Penn Station

She just kept trying to remember
the name of that *darling* little
French/Japanese place
in the West Village
where her and Sheldon
ate once on a rainy Friday Fall night
but couldn't
so she went on to describe
in graphic detail everything
they had eaten while
mispronouncing the dishes.

The Bounty Hunter Dog Wanna-Be
in the orange/yellow licking flames
stocking cap/black plastic wrap around
sunglasses/poor oral hygiene/on the 3rd day
of a weeklong amphetamine binge
bragging to everybody in ear shot
just what he told that Big-Shot Billy Joel.

Empty Suit 30- Nothing
making with the endless
smug prattle of pointless
power pointed business
related ego vignettes
designed to impress
in a Conservative talk
show radio commentator

VINCENT QUATROCHE

NPR tone of voice while
a fawning intern across
the table is responding to him
with wooooos & aaaaaaaahhhs
like Suzyn Waldman makes
while blowing John Sterling
in the broadcast booth between innings.

Infestation

Them Things are everywhere
We are addicted to them
Mechanical Vermin.
We ride on them.
We ride in them.
They ride inside us.
Mechanized Vermin
are hungry and thirsty
and the cost of feeding them
maintaining them
is always going up
exponentially.
Mechanical Vermin
are advertised
lionized
romanticized
on every media
every medium
24/7
We cannot live without
Mechanized Vermin
as they drain the world
they helped to create
and now self-perpetuate
their veracious appetite
to consume every
natural and unnatural resource
of man and nature.

The cost of sustaining
our addiction to

VINCENT QUATROCHE

the Mechanical Vermin
is destroy everything
Using everything up.
Creating a new Caste system

There are the rich who can
afford the cost without
a second thought
and then the poor
whose lives are being
impoverished and pulverized.

As for the Middle Class?

Try Museums
If you can find one still open.

Lost Hour Maria

For M

In the lost hour
I woke up just before two
to dance, change the clocks and lose an hour
in sixty seconds flat till three AM
all the time half awake
thinking about her that night
she showed up at one of my readings
on the arm of Billy Gas who
was in love back then
with a gal named Maria.

She listened that night
without a word
To the silly ass men lost in their beer ego talk
She had this quiet way about her.
Could take an hour and make it seem
to pass in a instant just by watching
you say what you might do someday
and she stayed back at the little brown house
off the woods and cemetery in the backyard.
Her and Billy slept in a big blue screened-in
tent with candles all night long.

And all the clocks in the world
couldn't make that night long enough
for them I bet.

In the morning
she climbed a huge oak tree
to cut the chains on a broken
wooden bench swing with

a pair of sharp needle nose shears
in her back pocket.
On the way down she torn her jeans
and skinned one of her knees
and I can still see the bright red blood
and hear her laughing about it.

And her name was Maria.

Later over coffee
she talked about her little boy
with the bright red hair.
Being an photographer
in the hills of Central America
Making a living selling the pictures
to the tourists while eluding the local raping gangs
and how she would love that
Billy Gas as long as she could.

She left in the morning with him.
Never really saw her again
or in the same light
that way
as that night

Sooner than later
She left him.

But tonight as I
change every clock
in this house and instantly
just lose more and more time
I find myself thinking
and not forgetting
about a lost hour Maria.

Her Oval Frame

I found her in the attic
In a dust covered rectangular
Cardboard box.
-I don't remember how it got up there
Abandoned on the false ceiling
On the former domestic's room
That serves now as my Prayer Tower office.

When I noticed the box up there
It was as if I had never seen it before
In the eighteen years we have lived
In this Polish Palace built in 1899.

I took off the lid sending thick dust
Clumps flying and there she was inside
Looking up at me.

An oval portrait of a young woman somewhere in her twenties
Taken perhaps seventy, maybe eighty years ago
The colors of her blue and white dress
And tone of her flesh washed like a water color
From a time when photographic plates
Were just being perfected.

She looked up at me with an almost
accusatory hurt expression suggesting
Why did you hide me up here for all these years?

Honestly I didn't remember if I did or not
Had no real memory of ever seeing the box before
Or if I did it was discarded up there forgotten in the move
Glancing at it briefly unable to throw it out.

So I took her downstairs
In the oval shaped image
Worn on the edges a placed her portrait
In a common rectangular frame in front of the bookcase

And now her eyes followed me around the room
With same sad searching expression.

I named her Dorothea
I don't know why
As well as the nickname Dolly
Came to mind.

And from then on that was her name
When I talked to her.

In this light now
There is little conjecture about my decision
You see-
I know her
And she knows me.

Perhaps all this now is merely delusional whimsy
But since I found her we pass the seasons together
Dolly and I

Sometimes I put her in the front window
To watch the Summer sunset or a Winter snowstorm
Maybe the rain in the Spring or the leaves swirling in the Fall

I talk to Dolly when I am lonely
And she answers with that soft muted expression
She is sure of something unspoken
And so am I.

You see there is this undeniable bond now
A sense of familiarity and belonging
The sense of being lost and found
And a promise I will never put her back in that box
Up in the attic ever again
And someday I will find her oval frame

7/18

Remembering Echinacea

They said on the package
These seeds are for the Fall
Where this old poem reverberates
In the dirt dreaming of flowers
Out of season.

Hear these lines
In the voice in your head
Cross threaded counter clock wise guy
Always just dim enough to try
And get the lid back on the jar.

Pandora would be so proud
To think a cyber citizen of the Terrible Now
Might still let loose holy hell
In this numb estrangement night
With a keystroke choke hold.

Blossom there you Moron
Your persistence of memory
Where they dug all their seeds in you
Only to disappear like a melted stop watch
Before they ever had the chance to bloom.

Visions of Kenny

(the next two poems are for TJ & Kim)

Kenneth on the New London ferry
Up on deck smoking a Viceroy

Thinking about Aggie watching
the white wake slice Sound
cross currents to Orient Point.

Same old story here-
Time to collect the family
The Summer all ready on the skids
Going back down to the red convertible
And popping the trunk as the Duck bumps the dock
Fishing out a frosty can of Narragansett
Out of the cooler with cubes still stuck to it.

Back behind wheel he takes a long pull
Off the smoke exhaling

Thinking-

As soon as I get off this-I'm headed right down to Turner House
And taking Nana for a ride- We're going to get lost
For a few hours and have a long talk.

The Unsinkable Agnes Turner

-For Auntie Ag

Agnes was my Auntie Mane like Rosalind Russell in the Movie
She came down to Greenport to Turner House in the Summer
From Quincy where she known as a tireless
advocate for endless community services.

I remember her
In the kitchen while pressing hamburger patties
With her bare hands from a big bowl of crimson chopped chuck
Molding them to symmetrical perfection
While saying to me to tell everybody that Auntie Ag
Makes the best hamburgers in the world.

And I would as she sang along to AM radio hit parade
In the hot July twilight kitchen with the
Sunlight streaming through the curtains
To *Hang on Sloopy* by the McCoys
Or *Down in the Boondocks* by Billy Joel Royal.

I don't anybody ever really knew the depth
Of that kind, energetic spirit she exuded
But even then I did.

And when the shit hit the fan at Turner House
Auntie Agnes in pink Curlers wearing cat-eyed Harlequin Rose
tinted frame glasses and the scotch tape to hold down her spit curls
would just light a Parliament and laugh

Singing along to *They're Coming to Take Me Away ha-haaa*
By Napoleon X1V
And dance.

6/2018

October Shorts 10/15/15

Somewhere a wind chime
Found its voice
Choking on Spider Webs

*

The S Sound

Summer severed season sigh Sunday
Sullen sandals & swords silent

*

Please Tell Me...

...you at least when down swinging
As the horsehide popped into the catcher's glove

*

Astounding heart of the line up

Merton-
Who stepping out of his bath was accidentally
Electrocuted by an electric fan

Would bat him like Gehrig

in the 3 hole-
Then @ clean up
Alan Watts of course- like the splendid splinter
However if the both struck out
Would have to go with the

Rachmaninoff- scoring the 7 year itch
and Marylyn Monroe over a subway grate
while DiMaggio watching pissed off thinking about
Arthur Miller writing/hitting it out with his ex.

Ode to John Dunn

-No....Not that one

So there he was this lost looking skinny kid
With shoulder length red hair looking as dejected
As if he didn't have a friend in the world
Smoking a butt staring into the tin ashtray
Alone in a booth in the Campus Center of Fraud University

So I'm watching him while I crack a fresh beer from
The six pack I just bought and for some reason
I thought what the hell?
Now I'd prefer a girl in this situation-
But you know he's much better looking
Than me and maybe he's an ass magnet.

So I go over and introduce myself
And gave him a beer
Turns out we have something in common
He's a son of the south shore
And what with me being a north forker
We had something talk about.

I ask- *So how do you like college?*
Shrugging he replied- *fucking sucks*
Same bullshit as high school-same kind of dicks and ditzy chicks.

Yeah I know I said agreeing with him,
I figured that out within a couple of weeks
Of being a freshman
(which we both were)

So what I did was go downtown to the bars

And made friends with townies
They know the ropes around here
And if they like you?
You're in.
Now of course they are mostly really twisted burn outs
But all the cheap beer, good drugs and hot chicks are
Yours for the taking.
He eyed me suspiciously
And asked-
What the hell happened to your face?
I shrugged- *Birthmark- just your standard Port Wine Stain*
And asked him *what's up with your upper lip?*
O he goes bit an electrical cord when I was a baby still crawling
around.

Cool I said.
Then I asked *so what are you doing later?*
He shrugged *nothing probably- I hate that fucking Dorm*

So I ask- *wanna go downtown?*
I know this joint that's a red den of Iniquity-
Special tonight is 5 Rolling Rock Splits for a buck.

And in the 50 years later
of fucking fighting and foot racing
We are still brothers to this day.

7/2018

New Year Shorts 2013

Calling it Quits

On the cold Lake Shore
on that Winter afternoon
Near the tail end of the year
Rather unprovoked
She declared
I'm calling it quits....

He nodded
Understanding completely
And remarked instantaneously

It is better to call it quits
Before quits call you

*

Grudge Instructions

Edna declared
I hold grudges...yes I do.
Ok I said
Why?
Better yet *how?*
And then I never even bothered to ask…
Where?

Her Alabaster Blush

He would watch her turn pink
as she would think
and when she did speak

her alabaster skin spotted
a crimson blush that
would leak
then gush
soaking her
from her top
to her bottom.

*

Solving Tornados

What's the best way to get rid of that pesky tornado in your life?

O you didn't ask…

Well I'm going to tell you anyway.

The next time that son a bitch comes around?

Hold your ground

Stand right there in the middle of it.

Look it in the eye

Defiant and unapologetic

Counting on it getting rid of you.

And your problem.

*

Uneasy is the Head that wears the Crown

Just got the word
That Julius Caesar
Had head worms.
Well…..no wonder.

Shoulda Coulda….etc.

What should have been
Seldom ever is
And fully realized
Till after
It never was.

*

Holiday Buzz Kill

Man….she had this special gift
For ruining Christmas
Like a string of lights
That burns out on the tree
Before you even
Think about the time
To take it down.

Sonic Aquarium

Your April ears kissed knelt in noon genuflection
Submersing you in the bottom of a sonic aquarium
Resounding first Spring day full sunshine in warmth
Everything was exploding in concussions
The mad bird frenzy fucking/ building nests upon the motion
Lights over the garage like incubators
Engines roar bad exhaust pipes somewhere
in hot pursuit sirens wobble
Bells chime as a crow laughs
From down the block children shriek
The sidewalks echo in basketballs bouncing
Towards the courts net less orange hoops
Submersing you in the bottom of a sonic aquarium
Your April ears kissed knelt in noon genuflection

4/15

Anti Social Media

Once in awhile it seemed when the seasons sliced change
She would wake up around 3am in her bedroom hot flash stuffy
Then sweaty sheets did this damp chill soak
Thinking just why in hell she ever let him
Video tape the two of them years ago doing it.

My god-how many times?
Once was too much
But dozens were more like it.

She had heard the horror stories
From some of her girlfriends
About how their ex-lovers had
Posted clips of some of their most intimate moments
On some amateur porn site
Devoted to revenge.
She dismissed the idea
Thinking he wouldn't do that
And eventually fall back asleep.

In the morning at work
Before anybody else was in at the office yet.
She would Google all related websites
Featuring that sort of fifthly vendetta
Skimming searching for him & her

But all she ever saw was just blurry strangers fucking.

After all of this time
She still couldn't get these thoughts
out of her head.

That bastard- she thought.
He knew exactly where to post them.

4/27

April Shorts 2015

Genderizing Kafka

Ok look-
Have your way-
He never fell under the bed one night
And woke up a monstrous vermin
She did instead
Turned up as a lady bug

And the family
Still
Did better.

*

Your Frozen Rope

Of silence
Ending up a lasso
In the center of a halo.

*

What did he say?

And he pursed his lips
Smirking like a rats' ass sideways
and said.....

*

The Vindictive Proof Reader

When's the last time
You looked a painting

And in triumphant satisfaction
Dismissed the work
Glibly stating
That's spelled wrong

Am I out of Costume?

She glared at him
And spat
Don't be insolent
He shrugged
Sorry
I was going for obstinate.

*

Who derailed you?

So you can stop giving that look
Like I was the engineer
Of your latest train wreck.

*

Literary Crime Scene

I write these flawed poems with typos and mistakes
In the shape of orange accident cones and if you want
To understand them?
You'll just have to cross the yellow tape
And take your chances.

*

Substance Abuse Diagnoses

She looked at him with clear disgust and said
You realize of course you are rife with multiple addictions
He replied- Well perhaps
But I like to think of myself well rounded in that regard
And btw I'd appreciate if you would lay off my hobbies.

1st Day of Summer

Solstice scimitar shaft
Slicing search torch
Gleaming longest burn
briefest pinnacle of light
declining seconds after
the descent commences....

The shadows start their
Encroaching erosion
Immediately....

Beware
Learn that lesson
From those who would
Build their world
On your ashes.

Who was stuck with Who?

Without a busted hymen as a kid
I went head first into every cunt
That caught my eye
In memory of being delivered
C-Section or so I was told

Never got the chance
To come with the biological delay
Have spent lifetime
Trying to get delivered the right way.

All humans get the gift of a birth
And owe a death on the way out
Having to deal with the truth
A breach birth in the old days was bad news.

Then there was the scarlet stigmata.
Harmless enough
But in Sparta
They would have planted your little ass
On the mountain side.

For that to decide.

All your lovers
Who pulled that hair trigger in you.
Heard that firing signal
from their nails/toes done recently in French tips to the goatee
landing strips below

And it's...................... *Pull*

Faces left on bedroom floor
Voices resound in your ears you can't shake
Memory like lost baggage
Returned to sender but
The dead letter office forwarded
All of it in the care of Bartleby
Cedric had a disconnected line.

Shatter that heart
You old sentimental fool.
Your memory awash lost drowning
In this masturbatory vision and sound
gone splatter abstract ejaculation
in the swallow end of the gene pool

Dance around these things all night
And speak carefully in public retrospection
All lionization and alibis come to the same end
So either shut up or don't bend.

Over pretending your past never calls you.

It comes down to this
Either he or she wishing
In some half dream just before dawn
they might of have done better
truth be known....could probably be
no worse off in terrible now
then to have been stuck with you.

5/7/15

June Shorts 2017

Professor Meltdown

And so sir would you like to explain to this faculty
Inquiry committee why you sprayed the class
With that fire extinguisher yesterday evening
During your lecture?

Sure-
Because they weren't on fire.

*

Cheap Dates

And they sauntered into the bar
Like a couple of two for a dime guys.

*

Look

All I said was I wanted to see her some night
Play her accordion naked.

*

Beware

The muse you lose?
Just might be your own.

*

April said Goodbye

In the rainy backyard two Cardinals
Through the kitchen window over
The washer & the Dryer they were using the shallow puddles
Upon the red bricks as little bird baths when he
Went right over to the other one and kissed her
Right on the beak.

How quiet is it tonight?

(for Richard Bruatigan)

How quiet is it tonight?
You can hear the ferns
Fanning the fires

*

Versed in Persuasion Gutted

In this shallow Shrine
Shine demuted shadows
Shifting in sound sand drifts engrains
Everyone so obsessed with all this
Getting *this-*
Only problem is?
There isn't any *this*

*

Happy Anniversary

After 32 years of marriage?

They coexisted like the Morlocks and Eloi

*

Kentucky Re- Fried

Listen

I want the old Colonel Sanders backs

*

Digging Cyber Caesar up

Friends- droids and citzenoids

Lend me your limited attention spams

So- You actually watch Naked and Afraid?

Sometimes

When I feel naked and afraid.

And am thinking of you.

Did You Know?

Silent film star Harold Lloyd who preformed all his own stunts
On the screen didn't have either an index finger or a thumb
On his right hand?

That Lene Lovich once sang w/ the Residents on Picnic Boy?

That a Cool April Twilight
Hangs color of upside down icicles
In overcast shadows?

John Do Passos never asked Samuel Becket
Why he cut that wire with the lawn mower
While thinking that North Korea is the size of Rhode Island?

That every time Siouxsie & the Banshees sang kiss them for me
On the radio he often failed to resist the urge to fly around the room
Like a whirling dervish?

And further more the only thing that could make him stop
Was a bitch slap from Nina Hagen singing Cosmic Shiva?

He never did locate that fourth blank black dice that
Fell & disappeared under the desk into another dimension
Like that little girl did in that Twilight Zone episode?

He had always wanted to ask her was the reason she desisted him
So much was his existing outstanding distinguishing extinguishing
    features?

Some men are content to shoot themselves in the foot or just put that in
Their mouth but he insisted on blowing his dick up first thing every
    morning.

When interviewed Chico Marx responded to the question of what
    he liked
To do in his spare time? He responded – *fuck & play pool.*

The Hit Man

For ML

A Buick Sedan crawled the Providence City Street
The April Sky was baby blue .
The air light and cool.
Perfect baseball weather.
But the man hunched at the wheel
Was in a different line up this Day.

His name was Maury (Pro) Leaner
Six foot two out of Brookline Mass
He was primarily a middle infielder.

Newspapers from Burlington NC to Walla -Walla Washington
All told the same story in the box scores.
This guy could hit.

Pro signed w/ the Washington Senators at eighteen
And was sent down to Rookie Ball in Erie Pa.
In 13 games he batted 167 and ended up
Enlisted in the Marines for the next two years.

When he mustered out in 1957 Leaner was signed on
A tip from a scout with the Milwaukee Brewers and
His contract sold to the Pittsburg Pirates a few months later.

But word was getting around
Pro could hit.

Pirates were keeping close eye on him.
Thinking if Mazeroski or Dick Groat got hurt
This earnest respectful talent kid might come in handy.

That off season Maury hit 400 in Nicaragua
During the 1959-60 Winter ball season.
But Pro was growing up and changing
He was cut from the squad for missing curfews
He picked fights with Cuban players and even a few Umpires.

Now the scouts still said the Pro could hit
But was developing a reputation as a player
Who was self-destructive and seemed to sabotage
His own success-

But the talent was undeniable
Pittsburg kept him around
But Maz never did get hurt
And won the 1960 World Series
With a dramatic home run to beat the Yankees.
becoming a folk law legend and he wasn't going anywhere soon.

Pro's path to the majors was now blocked
And at twenty six was middle aged in minor league years.

Was released by the Pirates in 1961
Ended up catching on with Macon Packers
All the ball players were either has beens or never were
And all on the way down.

Leaner began to play in another league
More lucrative and room for advancement.
His stats started to pile up here too-
Armed Robbery/carrying a concealed weapon
And the new scouting reports from the Brookline Irish police
Pegged him as cheap hood Jewish troublemaker.

Still he could hit
308 for the Raleigh Capitals in an independent semi pro league in 64.
Teammates remarked he kept pretty much to himself
Preferring to spend hours alone

swatting a suspended rubber tire with a bat
in the basement of the locker room.

Still on occasion he would do stuff few could explain
Like the time he smuggled a homeless hobo onto
The team bus with enough beer to last the 12 hour ride.

Next stop was Tennessee batting 357 for another ham & egg league
And bouncing checks, stealing hotel TVs to fence.

By now the baseball scouts weren't watching some much anymore.
But the FBI was.

You see Leaner's new teammates were cheap hoods with names
Like Red Kelly, Billy A and the games were getting more intense
And he was known to be considered armed & dangerous with a gun
    or a bat.

In 1965 Pro graduated to the big leagues when a minor league
Mobster named Rassumsuen who was suspected on turning informant
Turned up in a snow bank with a 38 slug in the back of the head
After spending an evening at Leaner's apartment
The investigation was on-going.

Word got around.
He was suspended from baseball by American League President Joe
    Cronin
Soon after that Pro rang the bell of another mark and when he
    answered the door
Took a swing at his head
With his bat. The guy survived barely.

This caught the attention of the Patrirca Crime family
The Boston Red Sox of the underworld.

They put Pro in the lineup in all kinds of hits.
His latest scouting report was that he had ice water in his veins

And could hit anyone without remorse he was put up against,

In March 1970 a Providence jury convicted Maury (Pro) Leaner of
1st degree Murder.
He was sent to the Rhode Island Correctional Faculty with an
    indeterminate
Sentence of 20 years to life.

By all accounts he was a model prisoner.
Could swat in the joint too playing the inmate baseball team.

In 1980 he came to the aid of a Correctional Officer
Who was being strangled by a cord by another Con.

The action was noted.
His Murder conviction was overturned around Christmas in 1988
When he was released Maury was 53.

Leaner and his wife headed west ended up in Las Vegas.
Pro had finally learned his lesson
Doted on his son-coaching him in baseball.

His wife died of cancer at 56
He never remarried

Maury (Pro) Leaner died in 2013 at 77.

The news spread around the baseball world.
And all his former teammates who had gone on to the Bigs
With names like Gene Michael, Ed Brinkman, Rich Rollins
Donn Clendenon Tony Perez, Rusty Staub, Steve Blass
Rico Petrocelli, Tommy Agee, Cesar Tovar, Roy White
And even Mel Stottlemyre all said pretty much the same thing.

Pro could hit.

6/17

Walter Matthau's Hat

Now I have this ratty, worn, ancient NY Mets hat that I practically
   live in around the house.
Would wager I have done everything a man can do in it.
Sometimes I forget it's even on my head and wear it out in public.

So I'm in the local Save-a-Lot yesterday morning over in the meat
   section.
Looking over the turkey parts and out of the corner of my eye I notice
   this
Guy in a crisp impeccable pristine Yankees cap over near the chicken
   livers
Shaking his head and smirking at me with a bemused condescending
   vibe.

So I saunter down to the pork chops and keep shooting him looks until
He has to directly acknowledge me and he says in a snide sarcastic
Tone-

So......You're a Mets fan

I deadpan him with this innocent pokerfaced and reply matter of
   factly...

O you mean this hat? Nah I'm a Walter Matthau fan- You know that
   movie
From 68 called the Odd Couple? Well he appears in a number of
   scenes with
This very Mets hat. I got this on E-Bay years ago-cheap- surprisingly
   they
Say it's worth a quite a lot of money now.

Of course now dude in the Yankees cap seems interested and rather
impressed.

You could see the dollar signs lighting up his eyes.
And he goes....*really?*

Sure- been thinking about putting it back up for bid soon- should pay
for my Daughters tuition
At college for a couple of semesters...

Abruptly ending the conversation... Tipping my hat to him walking
away
Mumbling under my breath. *So who's on First? You dipshit....*

6/2018

The Time Machine

Nixon crying over getting caught cheating at Checkers

Ford without plates

Reagan taking one for team Hollywood

Two in the Bush that father & son act of war

and then in the Terrible Now

We have the eloi and morlocks

awaiting Senate confirmation/

while 144 Characters later

tagged as being on the *Watch list*

an obscure poet in Roman persona non grata Vox Populi intones

if they insist upon bread & circuses

Perhaps we should eat the rich and develop our own illusions draw
our own conclusions

in a Jonathan Swift conceit

begging the question.... can we get that as a carry out order?

delivered by Chariot?

or maybe

just when he makes the trains run on time.

1/24/17

1984 2017

For Bernard Block

The Clock struck in Twitter time to post. POTUS adjusted his
   bathrobe and palmed his

Device thinking as he snapped off the remote on the telescreen
   snarling *time to teach those*

Idiots the lesson for today.

Sleep eluded him most nights. All six telescreen Hi def 48 inch hype
   cyber link realty blared on 24/7

The Leader had one in every room. All Staff had strict orders. These
   windows on his

Enemies were never to be off line

Sometimes of late he would walk the halls in the White House in the
   wee hours.

Even the gravity of his position was not lost him.

Thinking I have the codes- *is this what it's like to be God?*

Abruptly his teenage son burst through the door

Eluding the Secret Service detail-

Asking- *Hey Dad I have a question for you*

May 2017 Shorts

*

Playing Russian Roulette Cyber Phone

Six Chambers Characters only
One wants to hear from you
All the others are blanks

*

We are all we will ever have

And we are awash
With devices that want
No part of us.

*

We Saw Horse

Upon a rocking broken sky
Prompted up in-between
Suspended thunder heads

*

Man....unless...

You get your mug out of the jug
And your hand out of your pants?
You we remain just another aging pilgrim
With dubious aspirations
Who fights tooth and nail
Resisting any enlightenment.

*

Left at the dock

He was ruthless in his pursuit
To be a nobody
Proudly beaming upon the Warf

After he missed the Cyber boat

The Missing Beat Link

For Phil

In my mind's eye I can see him sitting in a midtown bar near Penn Station over near 34th Street around supper time in mid October of 1961

He's young and fresh off the train from Philadelphia in town to audition for a role in an off-off-Broadway play. He's nearly broke and nursing a stepped on flat draft and thinking he needs to find a job somewhere. Pronto. The jukebox is playing *I found my thrill on Blueberry Hill* by Fats Domino. By nature he's minding his own business despite some random glances from a blond down the end of the bar, Good luck with that he considers. I'm broke and not Elvis.

So then in strolls this tall dark haired man, shy with strikingly good looks. He's built like a college half-back with quiet good manners and sits down on the rickety stool next to him, orders politely a speed rack whiskey.

They exchange wary glances. Big man produces a small spiral note book, lights a butt and starts writing in it.

Phil sighs in relief. Well at least he's not another a-hole with some weird axe to grid

Lost in his own thoughts he barely sees the two other fellows enter the bar and surround his seatmate. One is an intense looking thin Jewish guy with curly black hair and thick horn rim glasses fronting wild eyes. His side kick is a strapping classic roman profile bruiser with a big booming laugh.

Their intense animated enthusiastic conversation is infectious.

Clearly they know something that nobody else in the bar has a clue about

Despite himself he finds himself eavesdropping till at some point when his glass has been dry way too long- The guy the other two called Neil -

Looks over at him with a big smile and asks-

Hey buddy- want a drink?

October 2015

Did you call your Mom Today?

(for Boni-Dot)

Mom called me Thursday night.

M: I have no phone, no TV, nothing. I'm on my cell phone. I can't get thru to cablevision. You need to call them.

B: ok, I'll call right now. I'll ...

M: they aren't there. Sure they are closed. Sons of bitches. This is awful. I can't believe this. I have my TV in my room. That DVR works. I'll spend my life in my room.

B: wait how can one TV work? I thought you said ...

M: oh that TV is wonderful. It works like a charm. Oh wait a minute a message is coming across my TV telling me of an outage. Ok bye

Click.

B: (I just got home from work btw) I'm thinking about it and thinking she has no phone. I desperately want to ignore this. I know I can't.

B: (gently) mom I think I will call cablevision.

M: do what you want. That's fine.

B: ok I'll ...

M: (click)

Fast forward. I get mom an emergency appointment. She has to be there from 10am - 8 pm. I do what I can you know? Her TV is out, no phone, no wifi I think, I don't ask.

Mom has plans to do her banking and shopping at 8:30 Friday morning. Most importantly she has no bread. This is a fucking crisis. Epic crisis.

All is well in The Terrible Now.

But it wasn't.

I can't get through to her the next morning. Phones were on the night before. I don't feel like writing that conversation. It's. Too much.

Friday 2pm.
B: your phone works!

M: (angry nasty mom is back. I'm sad)

Yeah it's now on for long. Make me wait all day. Can't get downtown because of the carpetbaggers in town. This is ridiculous making me wait until 2:00 for someone to show up. Now the guy is saying it's an electrical problem. I don't need the TV. I can save the money each month. $200 a month for the GD shit? The GD bastards. All my books I've read already. I don't need this.

B. Mom can he hear you? He's probably doing the best he can. Please he is trying to help you.

M. Don't start with me Boni I don't need your shit right now (on and on and on about foreigners taking our jobs and blah blah)

B. (Very scared and nervous) I' m so sorry mom. I hope they figure it out. Can you tell me if your electric company is coming out?

M. Oh sure he's outside on his damn phone. Here we go. Doesn't want to listen to me. Well I got news for him I don't want cable any more. Son of a bitch.

M. I have no bread. I can't make a deposit now. I have no bread!

B. (Carefully). I thought you were going downtown this morning at 8:30.

M. The bank doesn't open until nine!!! Don't you understand?? Why aren't you understanding what I'm saying???????

B. But if you went to the store at 8:30...

M. They were coming between 8 and 5!!!! You know this you set this up!!!

B. (Me thinking this isn't the best time to say it was actually between 10 and 8)

B. Ok mom well hopefully

M. He's back in. Let me hear him give me an explanation for their incompetence.

B. Ok mom I love you.

About 15 min later I call back.

B. Hi mom! How are you?

M. Well my TV is on and the guy is so nice. It's not his fault. He's the wiener after all! (Talks to the worker forgets I'm there and hangs up)

I take a xanax. Or two.

Transcription Boni Dot Fash

Procrastination Puss

Low Tone
Gulches gyp Gullies
Slow phone
Vultures footrace Buzzards

Passing an old Chateau
Where all the rodents in the rodeo
Remind us about civilization in tow

Tin Tents Tin Tents
Without dents
Or ventilation vents
Tin Tents Tin Tents

Where scampering rodents detect
Tin tents no dents
Just rodents fidgeting bents
With no dents
In the tents
Or in the rodents

Primates pick up the line
And listen for awhile
Then spin and spin
Out on the tile
Then shed their skins upon the tile.
Upon the tile but only for a little while

Miss the isle? Miss the isle?
Will the tactile missile miss the isle?
By a mile by a mile

Handpicked primates
Spin and spin only for a little while
Everyone on trail upon the tile
Tin tents tin tents tin tents tin tents
No dents nodentsnodents No dents
No dents under the tin tents
-Just hoards of scampering rodents

Circa 1979

Lost Nicknames

Tim (Eat) Clark
Ed (Wick) Pulse
Sylvan (Lucky) Ward
Ken (Hawkeye) Loeb
Tom (Stump/Rosy/Junebug) Yates
Robert (Big Daddy) Johnson
Chris (Scurvy Dog) Johnson
David (Gumbo) Verity
Allen (Hawk) Edwards
Dave (Diamond Dave) Brandy
David (Asa) Garner
Joe (The Colonel) Crenshaw
Paul (The Bounder) Gabbert
Reid (Monk/M-4/Chip) Mahaffy
Vincent (Vinny, Jim, Gleepo/Fast) Quatroche
Robert Gene (Iny) Aanestad
Jim (Fin) Finno
Jin (Tut) Tuthill
Mark (Eck) Eckheart
Mark (Whataaat?) Bamback
Robert (Bo Boon) Verostek
David (Bones) Puritan

Really, Really Lost

Sweet William
Little Jack
Barb-B-Que
Pork Chop
Short Dog
Chicken Head

Snuffy
Chubby
Gilligan
Murf
Zeke
And
Rod.

V.I.A.I 2.0

(*Very Important Abstract Info*)

She had the memory of a Goldfish.

Please note Gold Fish have an average memory of three seconds.

Porcupines are especially good floaters.

It kind of figures in some odd way.

After all water is as far as I know unpunctual

An average person laughs 15 times a day.

Most of us are not very average.

Never break *the heart of an octopus.*

They have three of them.

Ants do not sleep.

I think I sense some controversy here

Armadillos can be housebroken.

But it takes time.

As an Iceberg melts
it makes a fizzing sound.

Is that so? Well so does the earth as it cooks in orbit.

Betsy Ross was born with a full set of teeth
And historians do not believe that she
Neither designed or sewed the first American flag.

May Shorts 2018

Empties for the Tribe

My Redemption Center manger reports that he was rather both impressed and somewhat astounded that my monthly visits yielded such considerable volume of empty beer bottles in the original packaging, clean counted and stacked in surgical precision on the pallet. He asked- did you really drink all these? I indicated that I had. Then he tipped his Cleveland Indian Cap to me.

*

Designated for Assignment

So the Dark Knight refusing to go to the pen hits the bricks to Cincy. Never has been the same since that Model in Gotham designated him for assignment.

*

The Mail in May

The mail in May falls mainly on the estranged- *per se*
Summer in the morning
Fall in the afternoon
This evening where some lost season light
Spills from out from the Dead Letter Office.

*

The Puzzle Poet

I'm just no good without a lot of other people's pieces

*

Naked and Afraid 2.0

O I don't know
What do you feel like eating tonight?
Said the camera man to the producer.

Sure the maggots and ferns look good
But I was thinking Arby's

DW-40

Makes me happy
And it should you too.

*

Unseasonable

When May cools in the evening
After July took her- lock stock over a barrel
As the lawnmower binge went bulimic
Planting seed just so see them flower
I washed the bird shit & embossed sap
From unknown projectile seedlings
Adhered to the car in the driveway windshield
I resorted to using a razor blade
While smoking a butt.

*

All your Devices

Sit silent
Mute
No- They won't talk to you
But I will

*

Mozart & Me

From the movie "Amadeus"

EMPEROR: Well, Herr Mozart! A good effort. Decidedly that. An excellent effort! You've shown us something quite new today.

[Mozart bows frantically: he is over-excited.]

MOZART: It is new, it is, isn't it, Sire?

EMPEROR: Yes, indeed.

MOZART: So then you like it? You really like it, Your Majesty?

EMPEROR: Of course I do. It's very good. Of course now and then - just now and then - it gets a touch elaborate.

MOZART: What do you mean, Sire?

EMPEROR: Well, I mean occasionally it seems to have, how shall one say? [he stops in difficulty; turning to Orsini-Rosenberg] How shall one say, Director?

ORSINI-ROSENBERG: Too many notes, Your Majesty?

EMPEROR: Exactly. Very well put. Too many notes.

MOZART: I don't understand. There are just as many notes, Majesty, as are required. Neither more nor less.

EMPEROR: My dear fellow, there are in fact only so many notes the ear can hear in the course of an evening. I think I'm right in saying that, aren't I, Court Composer?

SALIERI: Yes! yes! er, on the whole, yes, Majesty.

MOZART: But this is absurd!

EMPEROR: My dear, young man, don't take it too hard. Your work is ingenious. It's quality work. And there are simply too many notes, that's all. Cut a few and it will be perfect.

MOZART: Which few did you have in mind, Majesty?

EMPEROR: Well. There it is.

You know? They say the same thing about my Poetry

Lost & Found June Fragments 2018

Wipe your Feet/Wash your Hands

So where the hell is he anyway?
Probably drinking himself into a doormat or down the kitchen drain
Check the Fridge
His face used to be on the Milk Carton

*

Hey Moe!

That last Poetry Reading?
He left them thinking
They just found
The fourth Stooge

*

Your Emotional Lottery Ticket

Just count yourself lucky
You never ended up with me
In the dark places of myself.

*

Drinking with Scratch and Sniff

Just itch and bottoms up

*

Preferred Bumper Sticker

Look —
If you want to ride my bumper
At least pull my hair

Everybody is a Critic...but

Yeah sure-

I might have been
So much cheap theater
But you had such good lines
In any other scene in your life.

*

Stock Market Relationship Crash

She was like money in the bank
That had already had a run on it.

*

Look

Nobody wants to hear it
But- They all still ask

*

Three Things to do with a Poet

1. Nod your head and smile begrudgingly
2. Kick some ass immediately
3. Kiss them and laugh

*

Millennial Job Performance Evaluation

- attributed to my son

In Brooklyn
Somebody always knows better
While at work in Manhattan?
It's- *what have I done wrong for you lately?*

What's Smatter?

I noticed you're alone tonight
You run out of arm candy?

*

Make Mine Ground Glass

What kind of bottle beer do you have?
The bartender rattled off the list-of course they had everything except
what he wanted.
He shrugged- *just bring me a draft of anything.*
Bartender came back with a tall pilsner glass and as he set it on the
bar it shattered.
Bartender went- *well I'll be damned.*
He said *o that's ok- I really didn't want that anyway.*

Cinema Paradiso

I was raised the son of an artist movie manager
In a deco-desperado palace built in 1939
Just are the hurricane of 38 leveled the former theater.

The role of my father was played by David Niven
By way of Robert Young
Mom was Ginger Rodgers/Kitty Foil blonde
And sold the tickets

The Projectionist was named Jimmy D as played
William Bendix- smoked Gran Habano cigars, read dirty magazines
And loved to fart and laugh.

The Porter was named Harold
A reclusive Boo Radley anti-social Savant
Who lurked in the shadows cleaning the
Theater at 3 am.

In my childhood on the Forbidden Planet
I rode in the Time Machine with the morlocks and the id monster
I cried when they sank the Bismarck
The life lesson of Gorgo and his mom stuck with me for years ago
And Spartacus was my baby sister.

Later
I worked there as an Usher
Playing myself
As a relief manager later on

The role of my love interest
Was played by all the women
Whose ticket I tore
And forgot my name.

But I still remember my time in the Cinema Paradiso.

7/2018

Double Think Indemnity

In the other room Edwin G. Robinson and Fred MacMurray
Are trading theoretical theories about the accident claim
Ed smells a rat.
Fred smells Barbara Stanwyck.

Fred and Barbara are in deep
Up to their necks
With the husband thrown from the observation
Car on the rear of that train to the tracks below

Fred is sweating out the truth
In flashback on the office Dictaphone
Confessing it all to Keyes-

As Fred is bleeding to death
He says I should have known better
This scheme didn't work out in
The Postman always Rings Twice either.

Just ask John Garfield and Lana Turner.

5/2018

On the Corner of Broadway and 39th

There is still an hour
Left to escape
Duck all this
Just walk down to Penn
And get on the 2:05
And rode out to the end of the Island
And head straight for the Sound
That you saw in your dreams
Last night so clearly
Pristine
Clear and transparent
As polished glass
concentric ripples
in the highest pure tide.

I could just stand there
On the bluffs overlooking
Where clean clear glacial stones wash
Whispering to each other
This Sound as it must have appeared
Hundreds of years ago
Before
A plague of plastic, rubber
Scattered junk yard
Of industrial age broken spare parts
And shattered useless fragments.

Nothing in the water but unadulterated Sound
Even the seaweed and jellyfish
All strained out
Just patterns of healing motion

Undulating peace and consolation

And I know that's what I should do
Even want to.

But I choose to ride the E instead to Queens
I have a carton of cigarettes to deliver
And paint your kitchen.

5/2009

Aftermath

Midnight just passed.
I'm in drained tatters here
after you left
about an hour ago
I've moved off the bed
exactly three times
to get three beers
The room looks like a sex bomb
was recently denoted in here.
The sheets stained with your mark
a perfect outline of the underside
of a vagina etched in dried cum
we both contributed to
most of the afternoon.

Your gone now.
Taking a cab back to another part of Queens.
Back to that apartment and him.

I'm pushing that out of my head
right now with all the might I can muster…
And it's not much…there buster…

I've been up now for over 22 hours…
So I get out my folder of timetables
schedules, phone numbers and start
to figure out where and how to keep a promise.

I need to pass out for a few hours.
Get up early and try and get this snarling chaos
of my madness in this room back into small
travel bags and figure out just what my next move

will be and just what the fuck it is I think I doing with all this.

But you're gone now.
I think of so many things I want to say to you right now.
The TV news shows a fugitive cop killer I'd like to discuss with you.
It's my hometown you see that
I was escaping from too as well to see you.

And now you're missing
from here
this shattered room
the ravaged torn apart bed
with the sheets soaked in dried seamen and sweat
I shrug at mountains of crumpled lust
and call home.

My wife answers
asking, *"How are you and what's new?"* *(She knows)*
"O...not much dear..."(I'm a worthless two timing bastard)
The conversation ends after a short time with reserved emotions
and polite *"love you"* goodnights.

I sit in the hotel room alone.
I bury my face in the pillow.
I smell your hair.
See your eyes shining into mine
from earlier in the afternoon
and drop off into dream
where I'm walking you
to your first day at community college

9/06

What kind of guy was He?

(collected)

What kind of guy was He?

What kind of guy was he?

He was the kind of guy
who tried to steer while
on the conveyor belt
of an automated Car Wash.

*

What kind of Guy was He? 2.0

What kind of guy was he?

Well when he finally took down those
Disgusting filthy filling station
hanging nicotine stained adhesive
Strips designed for flies to stick to?
He used to *count.*

*

What kind of Guy was He? 3.0

What kind of guy was he?

He was the kind of guy
That when he heard
Ice cream trucks
On summer evening
And all he wanted was

to buy somebody
One delicious cold moment.

What Kind of guy was He? 4.0

What kind of guy was he?

On a Fall evening
If his feelings got hurt
Because his wind chimes
Weren't making enough noise?

He would go outside
And smack them around.

*

What Kind of guy was he? 5.0

What kind of guy was he?

If you had to go to hell
On a train?
You could only hope he wasn't the conductor
Or worse yet the engineer.

*

What Kind of guy was he? 6.0

What Kind of guy was he?

When other teachers bragged
About their severance packages
And asked about his retirement plan?

He replied *death.*

Real Life Cyber Funnies lost
& found in the Spam

Guarantee > All dialogue is reported verbatim- Stan Mack
To be Spam..... or ......not to be Spam..............
That is the question....

*

Daily updated sissy blog there dude
sheet metal sales education for teachers
defining diversity driving defensively

*

So this your big idea underground website? Bro –no offense
here but you're just another vanity Blog. However get in touch>
I could make you big in Jovial / Bucuresti | Suntem un salon
de infrumusetare situat in zona Unirii (Bucuresti), care vine
in intampinarea clientilor sai cu servicii profesioniste de:
Coafor, Frizerie, Tratamente Par, Manichiura, Pedichiura,
Epilare cu Ceara, Epilare Laser, Barbering, Machiaj, Gene,
Sprancene, Tratamente Faciale, Tratamente Corporale.

*

The ceramic tile setters have actually installed the risers,
thus you'll have the capacity to observe the scene, however
we doubt you have the smarts, guts or where with all to
understand the nature of the gallows waiting for you

*

They are actually still incorporating the cement
with insinuation and insulation. Cyber Neighborhood disease watch
lives next door to theactions, will comply with the digital truths
certainly to uncover the building gates that are now fire-walls
defending cautions emulating from public usage and social view.
Meanwhile you stupid delusional pathetic bastard you think this
is encoded as a secret message to your enlarged prostate ego.

*

You could definitely see your enthusiasm in the paintings you write.
This sector hopes for more passionate writers like you who aren't
afraid to mention how they believe in pigment. All the time follow
your heart. Have you tried our scented lubricate? Just asking.

*

Well considering your limited talents & despite achieving
so much, there pal you, like all those who will pass through
this mortal coil, believe being beset with frustrations and
failures at times will endure and count as your legacy. You
could get them in different colors and alternate daily, or mix
and match for that Punky – Brewster look. Probably the
best you can hope for you delusional narcissistic cliché

*

Aw, this was an extremely poignant post. Taking
the time and actual effort to emote
to produce pseudo prose abstractions...
but what can I say... I hesitate
to criticize a lot but never seem to get
pretentious prose ejaculations

*

Mod Protrude
monster energy belt woman in prison transport cuffs
cell phone no & how come you never call me?

*

Your invited! Online dating for everyone Free nudist
personals in our on line church dating site

*

Consider this your notification. We're sending a letter to
the other side's lawyer as to this fact and strategy to
complain about your site to the state bar. Using
copyrighted material as references to write articles
is illegal. Expect to hear from our attorneys

*

We specialize in Van Gogh wall paper for true bathroom
decor masterpieces. Focaccia can be prepared in advance and
reheated or eaten cold as a snack. As a benefit. Fortunately,
California voters have a better choice. Personally, I even
bought a small canister of pepper spray for protection.

*

Your books are tiresome and overly descriptive & laborious.
Such unshared internal drama. For example, you might
say, "Wow, I really did great in that interview.
The runners traditionally wear white paints and a
white shirt, with a red scarf around their waists.

*As for the total effect I'm not sure if your personality
matches the book, but honestly, you seem as if you had
been trapped in the maze for years, really.*

*

*Dear Phony- You realize that your students don't even bother
to evaluate your old ass on rate my professor sites or facebook
anymore. But comments are all over twitter and the like. You
may think you're so impressive, but dude they dismiss you
in ten words or less. I specifically liked that one calling you
a crazy bastard who acts like a stern founding father but
they thought your daughter was hot was funny however.*

*

*I do love the manner in which you have presented this concern
plus it does supply me personally some fodder for thought.
Nonetheless, from just what I have witnessed, I basically
trust as the feed-back stack on that people today keep on
issue and not start upon a soap box involving the news of
the day. Yet, thank you for this fantastic piece and while I do
not concur with this in totality, I value the perspective.*

*

*Hey there! This post could not be written any
better! Reading through this post reminds me
of my old roommate who said he once took a course
from you! He basically said your were and asshole
but who was very kind to other assholes so he thought
you played favorites. He hated your guts.
I will forward this page to him. Pretty sure
he will have a good read. Thank you for sharing!*

*

*My mind was astonished when I've first seen this awesome
Rubber Eden. You become a frontline commando with your
guns blazing, while you snipe the zombie devils from Gridville
witnessing untold amounts of zombie bugs dead, trigger invariably
twitching as you launch your shadow gun while throwing image
grenades everywhere. Using only your Metaphorical end game
mythical ego kingdom and all on my very own android screen.
Best Rubber ever. Modern Poetry gets blended with murky
and pessimistic futurism, where your shadow Blunderbuss
Terrible Now always clearly indicates blow back or misfire.
Giving us only indescribable panic of having Eden occupied
by dead zombie bugs. Billions of them, in fact. All hungry for
our blood and our women! Cool ego shooter, hard Cat, wow.*

*

*I was recommended this website by my Ex, by way of
his therapist. I am not sure whether this post is written
by him as no one else knows about such detailed
info about my problem. You are wonderful!
Thanks! Jerk off!*

*

*Thank you for the auspicious write up. It if truth be told
you are such a used up an amusement park. Nobody really gives
a shit. Count on it, So take that adverted glance of yours and
drop dead all ready. By the way, how could we communicate?
Terrible new book now or otherwise, and that
one short story was only explained
in a most superficial way and once you reach
the end the reader is left nowhere
Do you write with of the eye patch or something?*

*

*Do you mind if I quote a few of your posts as long as I provide
credit and sources back to your weblog? My website is in the
general direction of the same batshit nothingness as yours and
my visitors would truly benefit knowing I'm not the only peculiar
self-absorbed narcissist pretentious train wreck lucking behind
a superficial persona as the supposed underground artist/writer
awaiting so some supposed benediction//validation of fame.
Please let me know if this ok with you. Regards!*

*

*Today, I went to the beachfront with my kid. I found a sea
shell and gave it to my 4 year old daughter and said "You can
hear the ocean if you put this to your ear." She put the shell to
her ear and screamed. There was a hermit crab inside and it
pinched her. I told her that's ok honey I knew this poet in college
who used to the same sort of thing with his supposed work.*

*

*My wife and I ended up being absolutely relieved when Ervin
managed to carry out his homework while using the ideas he
obtained through your weblog. It is now and again perplexing
to simply possibly be offering secrets and techniques that people
today could have been trying to sell. And we also consider
we need you to thank for this. The illustrations you've made,
the easy web site navigation, the relationships you will give
support to create – it's many fantastic, and it's really making
our son and the family imagine that the terrible now can be
interesting, and that is highly important. Many thanks for the
whole lot! But you do realize you were born quite mad.*

*

It's like you read my mind! You appear to know a lot about nothing, such as you wrote in that ebook or CD or something. I think that you just can do with a few percent to pressure the message home a bit, however other than that, this is magnificent blog. It's like you read my mind. Is it any good?. I will definitely be back. My Doctor says this sort of thing is a harmless recreational delusion.

*

WTF!? Clearly this is not a site with any rubber products. Was looking for some mud boots...And while we're at it here smart-ass..... Read your Bible.....there wasn't any latex bac in paradise. How the hell do you think you ended up here? I do. BTW you realize your f-ing nuts don't you?

*

Particular person baby..... the results of earlier pregnant pauses.... incredibly difficult to control or replicate... really should be expecting right back from students immaturity, inconsideration and also unpreparedness to manage tomorrow...and ok there professor were you any better when you were their age?

*

At least this shows you really care, since it's from the heart, it's probably a really good poem, and showing something really well written is better than showing something merely indulgent rubbish at any rate and if you're really not comfortable with this however, write something else so if you are not that especially talented try not to let the quality suffer. Perhaps you might give a thought to writing a poem about not wanting to show people your work. Be ironic.(Whenever you seem to hit a wall creatively, you can get around it by writing about hitting that wall. Or write about your frustration with the nature of the wall, it's a nice little trick that keeps it meaningful)

*

Begrudgingly I have to admit there is something to the strange, insistent goose step to your prose, but sadly if it walks like a duck, quacks like a duck and reads like strictly common fowl pathos? Orwell refereed to it as duckspeak. Ever consider calling your next book Quack & Ride? You are just another minor poet with a limited amount of talent and visibility. Perhaps you might trying flying south for the winter of your discontent?

*

Hi there, how's it going? Just shared this with a colleague, we had a good laugh.

*

Hey
Are you still correcting the posts of yours?
I've came across 29 grammar errors.
Lost count with the spelling ones....
And you teach College......supposedly...
Best wishes

You are so cool! I do not suppose I've truly read through anything like this before. So wonderful to find somebody with such unique thoughts..... Really.....thanks for The Rubber Eden. This website is something that is needed on the internet, someone with a little originality! Did you think it up all by yourself?

*

*Just a random question/suggestion here....So why aren't
you on Twitter? I can see your Hashtag now.....#asshole!*

*

*I'm an aspiring poet in school & I showed some of your stuff
on the website to my Creative Writing English Professor & she
said you had a sort of intellectual Crohn's Disease. I asked why
she thought that? Her comment was that writers like you were
a dime a dozen narcissistic hacks with delusions of grandeur,
relevancy or significance. I think she was being mean. She
acted like she knew you or something. Ever been to Peoria?*

Cheat Sheet for Crossword Poetry *from page 24*

<u>Down</u>

1. Angel Eyes
3. Sharp Corners
5. Zeuxis
7. Art
9. The Chain Gang

<u>Across</u>

2. Water
5. Talk
7. Ford's Theater
9. Curled his lips
12. McHale's Navy
13. Robert Plant
14. Godot

Down

13.Missing Persons

15. Peter Sellers

16. Yogi Berra

18. The Coal Yard

19. Verkhovyna (The Big Mountain)

21. Black

Listening to Bananarama in Tonawanda

-to be read while listening to Cruel Summer

Little Boy Blue
Come drink your beer
That cold slug down your mug
Makes you a Miller Time seer.

Thinking
Poor Herman Munster
Crushed by a dumpster
Poor ole Muster
Mushed under da dumpster.

So the heat in street
To the beat of the feet
Propelling the cars
Under the stars
Fill her up
And check that oil
Where's my spare?
In the trunk
Without air.

The freckled Bustard
Smothered in custard
Corporate thugs from Getty
Eager and ready
Laying on the propaganda
Thick and steady

Their slogan:
America is having the freedom

To be a rugged individual soloing
Down the rapid cataract
In a kayak in Nyack
Inna kayak in Nyack
Inna kayak in Nyack.
And it's a cruel, (cruel), cruel summer
Leaving me here on my own
It's a cruel, (it's a cruel), cruel summer
Now you're gone

Circa 1983

The Neutron Blonde

All was left standing
Intact
However
Nothing worked anymore.

Nothing rushed in the streets
Nothing flew in the air
Every screen and devise
Black and mute.

There was a red notebook
Left open on the kitchen table
The script still legible
With no one left to read it.

Once he talked with her
Face to face
Ending up with her gone
Without a trace

And she left all the buildings standing
And the cars stalled in the streets with their doors ajar
And the coffee in the cup half drank still steaming
And the dishes in the sink left undone
And only them left to look out the windows

And in a whisper remember

Just how alone
We all will be left
Someday.

THE LAKE AFFECTS

(Thanks Murph)

Sing in me
Through me tell the story
Of a four wheel drive
To Chautauqua County
Through a blizzard
Of name drops

Beside himself was
George Wallace
Fresh out of Long Island
By way of Brooklyn
He'd been reading with Robert Gibbons
Over cups of tea
And lager
In a bookshop

The snow came down somewhere in Pennsylvania
We avoided the traps of the Amish
And auto corrected slips
Like a Highlander
To witness a white dawn
Over the whitest town
Of which Groucho couldn't belong

There was no Hail in Fredonia!
Only snow and only snow and snow

Vincent Quatroche made arrangements to meet us
In a parking lot at some strip mall
That had not been ploughed
We sat infringed

To stretch your legs meant death
We breathed our watch
And waited for the end

There he was though after a while with some familiar smile
And a gathering was in
And a hotel on the edge of a lake
Where even the geese had purple feet
Or flippers
And we all relieved our gasps and bedded our sighs
To be
Just to be stationary
And then there was Phillip Giambri
The years melted like a hot toddler's impatience
To blow out those Carvel candles
We were all of a piece
The four of us
One for each decade after sensible
And where did we leave that sense
We left ourselves on a stage
Big dripping puddles of half formed
Imagined

As Hal Hartley said
There's no such thing as adventure and romance
There's only trouble and desire

So to the girls' rugby team that arm wrestled you into the night
To the invitations that kept coming
To Vincent Q's wife
To the cold winds of Buffalo
And environs
To again

Anthony Murphy (aka Murph)
(11/13/15)

Selected Poems from David Lunde

You and Vincent

Sometimes in the starry starry night
You and Vincent under the hollow
Craters of the moon sardonic
Watering the already early morning
Dew-sloppy grass with used
Beer, feeling comradely quite
Entranced connecting the dots
In the sky to make all the figures
Your Dads passed down all the way
From Babylon and you both with
Sons who will need that Knowledge
Someday entirely too soon so you
Turn each to find the other
Tugging at the lobe of his ear.

David Lunde 6/6/1994

A Greeting for Boni-Iris

Precipitate child, such a hurry
You're in already, so impatient
To leap from the tide-pool
Into the sea. Just remember
Whose hands were there to catch
You, little fish, and who
Kept you safe and warm
All that time when Winter
Chilblained the world, Now
It's your turn to cherish

Them in turn-yes that
Smile will do for a start
And remember to be kind and attentive to your elders
(and that includes big brothers)
Even if they seem to always want to spoil your fun
Playing wild porpoise way off shore.
Don't forget that your folks are long distance swimmers
Who can guide you around reefs and whirlpools
And who hope for the day that you will swim more strongly more
joyfully then they

David Lunde 6/13/1997

PRIVY

You think about where that fly lives, where he was probably born.
You think about what he's carrying.
How many diseases are there in human shit?
Not to mention the shit itself, which undoubtedly adheres to the hairy
    little feet
That are crisscrossing your ass, strolling over your balls.
You think about it.
You think about rearing up and whapping the little bastard good.
Maybe with a pad of crap-paper in your hand to keep the shit off it.
But you don't do it.
You sit there waiting for it to be over,
Straining just as hard as you can. While the filth-covered feet go on
    crawling,
And your flesh crawls too.
You think about swatting, but you don't do it.
You don't do it because sometimes it isn't a fly.
Sometimes it's a Wasp.

David Lunde 4/4/1993

Dreaming of Li Po (1)
By Tu Fu (712-770 AD)

Parting with the Dead
One eventually stops sobbing
But parting with the living
Brings unceasing sorrow.
Exiled to Yeh-lang in Chiang-nan,
Placed plagued by Malaria,
And no news of you old friend.
But you enter my dreams tonight
For you are always in my thoughts.
You are tangled up
In the nets of the law;
How did you free your wings
To fly here?
It makes me fear this soul
Is not that of one still living*
The road between us
Is too long to measure
When your soul came this way
You could see the green maples
But when your soul returns
It will travel through dark passages.
As I wake, the sinking, the sinking moon
Fills the roof-beams with light
And I stare about, half expecting to see your face.
Between us the water is deep
And the waves board and tall-
Don't let the water-dragons
Size you my friend! Circa 759

*Souls of the living were believed to travel at times of unconsciousness
But not as freely as those of the dead.

Translation David Lunde

Dreaming of Li Po (2)
By Tu Fu (712-770 AD)

All day long clouds floated restlessly
And still the wanderer has not yet arrived.
Three nights in a row I've dreamt of you:
I can see the kindly concern in your mind,
But you always leave in a rush
Saying ruefully, *Coming here wasn't easy-*
The wind blew wild waves on the river and lake
And I was afraid I'd lose my oars and capsize.
You go out the door scratching your white hair
As if disappointed in your life's dreams.
The capital city is filled with officials-
Why should this man be so wretched?
Who says the Emperor spreads a wide net
In his search for men of talent?
Li is getting old, and he is still struggling.
Making a name to last a thousand autumns
Is a pointless post-mortem affair.

Translation: David Lunde

Wine upon our Lips
Selected Poetry Passages
By Vincent Quatroche Sr.
1946-1951

For Joe Turner

Hey Pop

Hey Pop-
How's about splitting
This quart of beer
With me
It's hot a hell
It's July
The beer is icy cold
Hey Pop-
The grass is getting green
Over where you lay.

Circa Summer 1965

Untitled -*abridged*

I stirred the dust in an empty glass
A Rye and Ginger-bubbled effervescently
With globules of Moister running down the side
Unto the white table cloth

I was with you
Together once again
I felt your hand- cool and damp- slender
My thoughts spasmodic.

Now I am alone
I dance with a shadow
Drink with a shadow
Neither seeing or hearing
Since I kissed your lips.

Your shadow and mine
Another cigarette
Another drink
I draw odd shapes
On the wet counter
With the mixer
And think
Endless detached strings of memory
Tonight
Tomorrow
And after that last night
Nothing will ever be the same..

Southampton August 12th 1946

Seasonal Mediation

We are but
Each of us
liken to a bud
a leaf
green with life
then
brown with age

We fall
And see no more the sunshine
Raked into piles
And burned

Sweet aromatics
About my nostrils

I breathe you deep
Into my soul
As I contemplate
The endless cycle
That is life

Wine upon our Lips-*abridged*

My lips sought yours
Across your naked forehead
Titled eyes
Upturned nose
Sensuous lips
Opening to join mine
We loved
With all the warmth
And our living flesh
We plunged deeply
In the joining
And drank the wine
Sweet upon our tongues

Is this flesh a barrier
To a greater joining
Beyond the physical
Is there a greater happiness
In another deeper union
Beyond this flesh

I am no Sage
No Prophet
I cannot answer these questions

Last night
The moon fell upon the sea
Touched each wave
Upon the tide
Each sand crystal
Each blade of beach grass

Fell upon your face
Your upturned nose
Your sensuous lips
Opening to join mine
We loved
With all the warmth
And our living flesh
We plunged deeply
In the joining
And drank the wine
Sweet upon our tongues

Circa July 1946

Next time I see you again

I'm reading your poetry Dad
Drinking a beer sitting on floor
In front of the fan on a hot
Waning June twilight.

On the pages you are twenty-five years old
Freshly mustard out of the Air Force after WW 2
Chasing tail on the ocean beaches of Southampton.

I hear your word resound from the page
As an I'm anold boy now but the message is
As clear as something I might have written
At the same age as you.

You were still a full 5 years away from marrying Edna.

Your passion and gift for life's sensations
Of the fire of youth was like hearing
Dizzy Gillespie and Sonny Rollins
Playing *The Eternal Triangle*
On the radio in the background.

And as I light a Camel with your Air Force Zippo light
I found in your box while looking for your poetry
And brought it back to like to spark
For the 1st time in sixty years I'm thinking

Hey Dad- the next time we meet
Let's both be young again and great friends
Like we always were.

6/2018

The Stars of Lid

For the daughters of quiet minds C & A

On the morning of the first class of the semester
At 8 AM she appeared at the doorway in the front
Of the room and announced in a general question
To all the students-
Is this COMM 155 Rhetoric of Vision & Sound?
Collectively they indicated it indeed was
And she exclaimed emphatically *YES!*
Pumping her fist in the air.

Within a week or two after class one morning
She approached the desk as I was packing up
And told me who she was and who her mom was
and what her Aunt (your sister) laughingly
said about you being in my class.

Pure synthesia and serendipity in the glorious revelation
I was looking at your daughter in my classroom
So when I asked how you were-
Her face darkened and told me you were in Hospice Care
And all elation of the moment was instantly deflated

Later that night with after work beers I was thinking of you.
Some 40 years ago when we met and spent some time together
I doubt it would qualify as even a minor affair
We never dated
But I still remember from the 1st time we met
Every time you were back in town
Wordlessly we spent all our time together.

From all the scattered fragments of those days

One still stands out
We were in the kitchen in my apartment in the early evening
Trying to explain to each other about being damaged and hurt
By others we thought we were in love with.

That night?
I remember holding on to one of your braids
As we slept together.

We drifted apart eventually
But I recall being told that you had been in town one night after that
And circling the block in your white Volkswagen
Looking for me on Antelope Street at 3 in the morning
And that still haunts me to this day
How I wish you had found me
And walked in the darken bedroom like dream.

That Semester was a tough one for your daughter
Some mornings I'd discover her with her head down
On her desk in the darkened classroom long before class would start
When I would arrive early.

I sent you a collection my short stories
They told me that others used to read them to you.
That made me very happy.

You didn't linger
You were gone well before the semester was over.
I knew without being told when you passed in late September
A couple of days later on a weekend night in October
I was in the kitchen drinking beer and listening to the radio.

And you were there with me for few moments.

I never told your daughter about any of this.
I thought maybe you might not like that then
But I want her to know now
And you too
How much you were loved.

7/2018

A
Life Sentence
One
Day at a Time

Just another Day in Paradise

Selected Poems From
14 Years teaching the Chautauqua County
Jail
Mayville NY

For All Those Doing Time

Winter

In this factory and prison winter
In the factory
In the prison
In the winter
I am the factory
To the winter
In the prison.

I hear stories at night
next to the booking desk.
The naked fear in her voice,
the resignation of her explanation.
Too young, too pretty, too much trouble again.
And she said she told the lady on the phone
that her kid is home alone.
But it's not like the movie, or being with
television cops who parole you with every commercial.

I walk by the trap at night
and give it a quick sideways glance.
It's between protective administrative isolation
and day care's "time out".

I talk softly in the little house.
So what else would you like to know?
I work in the factory.
I teach at the jail.
I need to get drunk
but never throw up in a pail.

Yes this is my natural face
no I didn't fall down

but my occasional lucidity
I did frequently quite successfully drown.

But don't swing into verse here
on my account.
It's just a factory
or a prison in the winter.

So wish for a cab.
and a fare to beat later
because beer break is over
the clock beats away on the wall
and your sentence is to have to look
for one good sold riff in all this
winter
all this factory
all this winter.

Can I remember my dreams
in this winter of factories and prisons.
Do my time.

To record:
The ghost trailing full on the tail pipes
like a little kid trying to keep up. The morning had an odd lot
certain puddles about the gutter like holes
or mirrors dashing reflections in front
of cars like terrified cats thinking
"If only I could get to the other side."
Last night I drove home from the prison in a thick fog.
Each street light cut a cone going down
shafts that poured a dirty wet yellow
in funnels of light cut inverted into the blackness.

I watch the sky brighten each dawn
and
heard the sound once in a green room
while three metal vats hummed or chanted or groaned
in finely ground Polypropylene.
At least I could sing along, at least to that.

But I only heard it once.
You sing that factory
So near the prison
in the winter.

I can't call you
out of the factory
so much like the prison
is the winter of our season.

To walk out in the dawn
I hear a heavy door swing open
here is your common release
some sort of parole
from winter in the factory.

I remember starting this in blackness
a silent icy blizzard of interment.
Now the dawn fire cries gulls
The sky is a blush broken vase of color.
I have gone from the darkness into the light.
Still winter and spring bicker over the factory
They long to dance, but struggle to let each
other lead or leave or arrive and the wind
howls one seasons name and sky writes the other
and in this confusion
there is this glorious donnybrook of light.

I will walk out today
into another ending.
I have made the transition
from a curious disfigured stranger to
that "pintaho" who used to work here,
that supposed "teacher" who thought himself
too good to work on Saturdays.
Now as the grey people scuffle past
mumbling in a foreign tongue
hissing hard glances at six a.m. to face
another ten hour day of tedium and drudgery.
I feel little save the distance approaching
rapidly between our lives.

This grey street will evaporate this afternoon.
My parking spot will open up forever.
Upon exiting the factory
my footsteps will not echo.
I leave nothing here
except a punched out time card
like a brutal sweaty map tracing ordinary toil.

Today I vanish from their harsh world.
My simple March into April's escape
where I still hope to be able to dream
and try to remember my time.
In the prison
In the factory
of this winter.

3/29/96

Saturday Afternoon in the Can

After I make out the class request sheet,
After I check the Alpha list in the booking room
for the block number on my incoming charges.
They move them around from cell to cell,
more than you might think, the usual squabbles,
Just can't seem to get along with the neighbors.
Just can't seem to crap on the open bowl, not really
in the center of the room, but partitions never were
part of the floor plan, so it would make you take less
on your tray and probably seldom ask for seconds of
the brown stuff.

The C.O.'s bringing them down the hallway.
They walk inmates, but sit down students,
so quickly and almost always get down to work
pretty fast. Their books, papers and pencils
all laid out for them, it all happens pretty fast
they always seem to want to get into it, to maybe
escape for an hour, like if only they could get back
to being in school and maybe that time before when
everything was all right.

A second chance to escape all the trouble.

I walk about the tables to answer any questions.
After that I turn up the small black radio in the corner
of the room up ever so slightly so that we all can hear
the Benedictine Monks singing in Gregorian Chant
"Christus Factus est pro Nobis".

4/96

Tuesday Night Lesson Plan
at the Little House

Tonight the guards brought Raffy in the classroom

with the side of his face blooming in fresh strawberries,

one eye so bloodshot it looked like a city street map

of Scranton. He smiled at me as he sat down to his workbook

and when I didn't ask (I never ask) Raffy simple stated,

"little disagreement up on F block."

Giving him a pencil I wondered out loud if he would be

O.K. to read

Raffy looks back at me and smiles from his freshly

detonated face and says, "Hey, I've got two eyes."

6/96

Bar Without Matches

Most of the boys in the can
don't really seem to belong
in there.
I see that if you take away a man's
beer, cigarettes, matches, woman,
children, drugs, money, wallet, street clothes
and dress them in hospital pajamas with their
naked feet in flip flops they are just like
everybody else.

Such a wide collection of sad eyes.
The ones that really get to you are those who just
don't talk about it. Ever.
No hard luck stories, no ever-present alibis
just all of them sitting around the table
discussing the weather like just like plain folks.

Today they brought Graham into my classroom
under six-inch leg shackles and what appeared to be
a fairly new set of handcuffs.
He shuffled in and nodded his head affably in my
direction. I had the urge to ask, "Hey, what's up with
all the jewelry, Bud, you trying to make a fashion
statement?"
But this wasn't a George Raft movie.
I don't play around in here.
When I see him under double lock down, I don't wonder
what he did, I think more along the lines of;
"Gee, I'm glad at least the ankle and wrist bracelets are
metal, not those suck ass plastic ones they use these days
to bind a man off like he was a big black baggie of garbage.

I'd hate to have to wear a pair of those plastic bands.
It would be like drinking shots of Dewar's in little
disposable medicine Dixie cups.

I never did ask Graham about the bracelets.
It just wasn't any of my business, after all you
don't ask people on the street why they wear the kind
of shoes they do.

I walked over to turn down the Strauss on the CD player
and Graham looks up and says;
"Oh, leave it alone, it was so refreshing."

5/96

Chet's Pal

I went down to the booking room
to get the fresh cell block assignments
for the night's class from the Alpha list.
As I pass the isolation box
I hear my name being chanted
over and over.
This is hard.
His voice resounds from behind the bars.
None of the COs even looked up from their duties.
(Except one latter matter of fact wisecrack
from the desk Sergeant, "Old Flame of yours?")
Evidently the COs had him warehoused in the
"Box" awaiting transport to the psychiatric ward
for "stabilization."
On the way passing the box I stick my neck in the doorway.
I know I'm asking for it.
He leers at me full blown Aqualung/Rasputin insane
spitting out, "You Fucking Bastard", He screams,
"I know YOU, your NOTHING,
but a MUTHERfucking Yellow COWARD. In fact you're a PURPLE
MUTHERfucking Coward TOO!!!! I've walked around in your
life and if I see you on the street next time, man I'm
gonna TELL you so!!!!"

The tirade spewed forth. I exited the corner
toward the elevator. I could still here him cursing
at me, ranting my name, even after
the pneumatic doors slid shut.

As I rode the elevator up to the classroom I thought;
O.K. Let's review, I'm on the radio ten years ago on

a Sunday afternoon playing Jazz and this guy calls me
up, full of claims about hanging with Chet Baker and
them sharing a woman and having all these unreleased
tapes of Chet playing and I did I want to hear them….
Well of course I did. I interviewed him, did a show
around the material and really that had been that…

Now as I unlock the door to the classroom I think some
more "you know, I wonder what his old friend Chet would
think about all this and if any of this guy's stories about
tapes were pirated from somewhere else in the first
place?"

Got to admit it. It got to me.
I asked the Shift Sergeant what the story on Chet's pal was.
"O him", Sgt. goes, "he's been slipping down for about a
week now, they're getting ready to "rubber room" out at
Lake Shore. Hell, I don't know…we weren't trained for this."
Then he smiles. Looks at me and says,
"So what's up with you? That's your second old friend up
here this month. You go to expect this after all this time,
your just having a "bumper crop" of "old time used to be

It happens. From time to time. They're going to turn up.
Considering your past which you keep pretty close to the
vest. It's simply the law of averages…after all
it could happen to you."

Driving back down the hill after work.
I'm still thinking about it.
Maybe I'm a little embarrassed. A little pissed off.
All that verbal abuse and madness blind sided
A La Cart, just today's special on the "Little House Menu"
There was more than a kernel of truth, in what
they all had said about me that night,

but if you put all our roles together there
was barely enough to make a decent sandwich.
Which I ordered pronto with a cold one.
As the radio in the back of the bar played,
Chet's long, thin sad trumpet notes from a
1958 recording called,
"It could happen to you."

6/2000

Welcome Wagon with Flat

-for Steve

Sometimes on a night like this after work
I say to the bartender,
"You know, once in awhile
after I punch access code
into three keyless lock pads
to leave the jail,
I wonder what it might be like
NOT to be able to leave the jail
and come down here and get a cold one."

I think
How about him?
He sits up in D Block.
Not going anywhere tonight.
Not going anywhere for a stretch.

I asked the shift Sergeant.
He said the same thing they all say;
"He looks pretty bad"
followed on the heels of;
"rode hard...
...put away wet."

I think.
"Well, hell that makes sense.
Four long years in Texas on the lamb
living on hardscrabble shoe strings
Always looking over your shoulder."
And then one day...BAM!

One routine background check later
and your cooling heels at the County's expense
Warehoused in the block iron rest home.
Shift Sergeant said;
"Want to see him?"
I said, "Yeah…but I really don't know what I'm
going to say…
other than…
what they all say,
"rode hard…put away wet."

6/00

Life Sentence, One Day at a Time

(for Sgt. C)

So you do a year in the can
so fast where there is hardly time
to wonder over the icy roads
the approximation of applying the brakes.
Going into the white-out for three
distinct ordinary horrifying five counts.
On your way to the jail
with the promise you'll make bail.
To reduce this sentence to lines falling off the pages
to stand up like bars of adverted adverbs
doing a life sentence
eight hours at a time.

Time to tango with all those uneducated eyes
blocked ears and tangled tongues spitting out
odometer readings like freshly shattered teeth.

A year in the can.
Tonight.
All that ties the dreams between
the releases and incarcerations.
Have a beer with this repeat offender.
Wondering where is all the color?
Seen any flash around here lately?
I check the clock in the booking room
watch its hands proceeding in double lock,
all the shapes and textures of this place
immured all across its face.

I'm working in the structure of order.
Tightrope over chaos, the very fabric that holds
society in its tether together.

A year in the can.
Arrested.
Removal. Warehoused. On ice. Stored. Penalties o plenty.
Pay the piper.
Pay the jailer.
Pay up.

I missed the payoff when he said it was time to seize
the torch. In the past, I found myself always
grabbing the wrong end.

My Sergeant. One tough bird.
A jailer's jailer.
Once told me a rough story.
Once an ex-con moved into the upper apartment,
just next store. He was a drunk.
He found out what the Sergeant
did for a living. Showed up at his doorway, smashed
as usual one night screaming, "Attica, I did time
in Attica and your little jail isn't shit."
Sergeant let it go. So the ex-con takes off with
it. Pulls the same routine at every opportunity.

Finally one time, enough is enough.
The Sergeant marches over the con's house and say's
"O.K. c'mon your going down the bar with me."
They walk in. The bartender comes. Sergeant orders for
the both of them. So here comes the beer. Cold, big
white head over golden body. Ex-con reaches his hand
towards the glass. Sergeant grabs his hand by the wrist.
And says…" hold it right there, you stupid son of

a bitch, You and me are going to have it out, get a
few things straight. Eyeball to eyeball, I'm not fucking
around with you anymore. Your going to cut the shit
or I'm going to find a way to make something stick and
then Mister two time loser your going away for a long,
long time. Get it? Now.......drink your fucking beer.

Ex-con cools out. Somewhat. Towards the Sergeant anyway.
Still it's not to long before he screws up. Tries to burn
down his ex-wives apartment. Looking at an arson rap.
They haul the ex-con to the "little house" and park his
ass pronto waiting for transport up state.

Ex-con dries out in the can. One night Sergeant shows
up in front of his cell. Staring at him. Ex-con figures
his ass is grass. Sergeant shakes his head, throws him
a pack of ready rolled, and says
"here, looks like you could use these."

Two years later. Ex-con gets sober. Gets religion.
Learns a trade. It sticks on the outside.
Gets a straight job. Shows up at Sergeant's door.
Hat in hand. All humble, full of how sorry he was for the
way he acted. Thanks Sergeant for not kicking him when
he was down and hands him a pack of cigarettes.
"Sir" Ex-Con goes, "that gesture of kindness that
night might have saved my life. I just wanted to stop by
tonight and give you these and say thank you."

Sergeant looks at him, say's "fine, your still an
asshole, now you got thirty seconds to get out of my yard
or I call a cruiser to pick you up and take you home.
Where you belong. Back in Jail.
A year in the can.
Drawing a paycheck.

With your own keys to the side door.

Teacher, Jailer, bail bondsman
The fingerprints, the handcuffs,
the mug shots, the rap sheet.
Year after year in the can
How many sentences?
One square deal, one square person to grab you by the
ears, maybe shake em, maybe box em
but they can tell you the truth
or trump,
skipping the trick.

2/97

More from Saturday Afternoon in the Can.

Today second shift shipped
my most promising student
into the classroom complete
with resplendent split lip
and the puffy angry purple
of a dawning shiner.

His relocation from private accommodations
in the Pods to N block
a change in apparel apparent
gone were the privileged tans replaced
with the more common greens.

It was very business like
No discussion was forthcoming.
He simply looked even more
determined and focused as ever
upon his goal.
Get that GED in the county jail
in April now that the prospect
of early release "good time"
was all shot to hell.

11/99

A Pause with the Warden

At check out time
in the hallway
near the visitor's entrance
I ran into the Captain
in front of the CO's mailboxes.

We locked eyes
and had this brief
exchange centered
around the subject
of the expression of stress
the relative nature of freedom
and the fragile element
inherently contained in
the thread of the consequences,
that one must carefully consider
while struggling to recognize
the identity and dignity
of all those whose lives
we had been entrusted with
on a regular daily basis.

Again as I had said
the exchange was brief.
But we agreed upon something
in those few moments
eyeball to eyeball
something understood
unsaid about the nature
the final disposition
of all our cases.

3/04

Weeping in the Walls

I was in the can next
to the jail classroom
taking a leak
and I could hear
the sound of
her muffled crying
bleeding through
the concrete blocks
from the women's section
just on the other side.

She sobbed, "I do want to die"
It was a heart breaking.
She sounded like a
ten year old kid
trapped in a very bad place.
A nightmare
she couldn't shake off.

I stood there feeling
a few things;
Pity
Horrified
Fascinated
And employed.

I shook.
zipped up
and the automatic
censor on the urinal
flushed.

And God
of course was fast asleep
dreaming that
all his children
clearly understood
the nature
of their
redemption.

Winter 96

Short Sentences

His eyes were the color of rare roast beef.
His teeth Indian corn yellow grinned as he said,
"After all it's not like you're doing time,
more like time is doing you

*

As the CO lead the group of students away from the Computer room
He made this snide remark about everyone now being all
    "edge-a-ma-cat-ed.
And I heard a female inmate reply, "No…but he blessed me with his
    sophistication."

*

I keep my keys to the various doors
of the jail on a length of
metal chain clipped to my belt.
The business ends lay in my pocket
Like a rosary beads of incarceration.

*

I usually can tell from the second
I pass through the third lockdown door
That inside here today the world's going to look
Like it has been shaved by a drunken barber.

*

CO had her on ice in the new trap.
She had on the blue suicide dress

And I couldn't help thinking about
Being all dressed up and nowhere to go.

*

Fresh up from Florida
Visiting her three kids
With three different fathers
Before her 22nd birthday gets popped
In a strange town with a bench warrant
And now with way too much youth
Still left in her face, you have to wonder how
That much life could be consumed in such a short time 02

Booking the Centipede

On my way to checking out
of the Clink one afternoon
I walked by the temporary holding cell
and took note of about roughly half a dozen pairs
of adult footwear scattered on the floor beneath
the plexi-glass window;

There was quite a variety.
Dirty sneakers, beat up cowboy boots,
scuffed loafers, muddy work boots
and somehow one odd white golf shoe.

I knew from experience
that the jail had just received
a fresh influx of clientele
from the local court systems.

They all needed to be processed.
They had been dumped in there
right at shift change time.

The Correction Officers just coming on
duty really hated that.

So I'm riding the elevator
to get out of there for the day
and it fills up with COs headed
to work and the one guy remarks to the other,
"Looks like we just got a new bunch in the back door"
"Yeah I know" his co-worker sighs with disgust,
"saw all the God Damn shoes in the hallway.

I elected to interject;
"Hey maybe their booking in a centipede, today"

Nobody laughed.

We all just looked down.

At our shoes.

11/06

Visiting Hours are...

Looking around
is never a real good idea
when you walk into the waiting room
area of the jail on your way into work.

Yeah. They see you.

So really you want some direct evidence of that?

Exchange a little suspicious eye contact.

You know why they are there.
Then can only guess who you are.

So you just keep your profile
pointed straight ahead.
Let them guess away.
Why this guy
appears to have some secret code to get
through those two steel locked doors
in get in.

Not only that
and then
he looks like
he just might
know how
to get his own
ass out.

5/07

153

Beautiful Day in the Neighborhood

On a June Saturday morning
I walk into the booking complex
to get the day's updated Alpha list
for the GED Students cell block assignments
and there is a semi naked inmate clad
in an adult diaper in the rubber room
screaming at me from behind the Plexiglas
every time I walk by to the copier.
He's screaming at me….***HEY…..HEY…..YOU…***
Now I know correct protocol in this situation.
No eye contact. No acknowledgement.
He's in where he is for a reason and so am I.
But I have to pass by him again on the way out
and again he starts screaming at me…

HEY….HEY….YOU…..DOCTOR….DOCTOR!!!

Again I'm just passing through here….head down towards the door…

So he adds……… ***FUCK YOU!***

I walk down the long sterile corridors thinking…but I'm not a doctor,
I don't even play one in the jail, I'm a teacher here and immediately
start singing the Mr. Rodger's Song.

I can do this.
After all
He was the one shooting the Anti-Freeze.

6/08

154

Creative Sentencing

In the stuffy silence
of the jail classroom
I sat arrested
incarcerated
gainfully employed
having been sentenced
to concurrent confinement
for the crime of being a teacher.

I had no lessons plans
knowledge or wisdom
to impart.
I knew nothing else
other than the access
code to get me outside
the lock-down doors.

The uniformity of punishment
was handed down
for all here on earth
without
prejudice or parole.

I was just simply allowed
to serve out my sentence
in another location.

Out of all the inmates
in the room that afternoon.
knew he was the one who
looked worse for wear.

They all looked and wondered
just what in hell had happened
to him.

The crime was always
one of the flesh
and verdict always
guilty as charged
and the only other
variable was after all
sometimes the sentence
wasn't all that creative.

6/20

V Formation

for Wayne

When I walked off the elevator onto the 1st floor towards the classroom
right next to the Woman's section I passed him sitting
in his chair in the cramped, cluttered Sergeant's station
office staring into the computer screen....

I hailed him.

Hey Sarge, how's it going today?

He barely looked up keeping his eyes on monitor.
Mumbled a per functionary acknowledgement.

I figured he was busy.
Maybe working on the CO duty rosters.
I knew how complicated that job was and how it aggravated him.
Decided to just pass by, opened up the door to the classroom
and head down the hallway in.

I heard a voice call after me.
Hey bud, you got a sec?

Sure I called back turning around and walked into the office.
He still didn't look up at me.

He said, watch this will ya?

On the screen was an animated colorful graphic of a black finely
    etched
silhouette of a flock of geese flying in a V formation across a Winter sky

157

at Sunset with new age music in the background.
Scrolling down across the screen were the following words:

As Each goose flaps its' wings it creates an "uplift" for the birds that follow. By following the "V" formation, the whole flock adds 71% greater flying range than if each bird flew alone

When a goose fails out of formation, it suddenly feels the drag and resistance of flying alone. It quickly moves back into formation to take advantage of the lifting power of the bird immediately in front of it.

When the lead goose tires, it rotates back in to the formation and another goose flies to that point position.

The geese flying in formation honk to encourage those up front to keep up with their speed.

When a goose gets sick, wounded or shot down, two geese drop out of formation to follow it down to help and protect it. They stay with it until it dies or is able to fly again. Then, they launch out with another formation or catch up with the flock.

I was astounded. It was a beautiful message. The very fact that this tough old Correctional officer Sergeant who had a reputation of being one no-nonsense volatile SOB, given to rages and shouting matches with those under his supervision over perceived incompetence or abuse of inmates was showing me this message. He had zero patience for fools, boot-lickers or ass kissers. We had always gotten along. For some reason he always looked out for me. He became my first friend in the Jail. He even fixed a speeding ticket for me once I had got heading to work without me asking. Just snatched it out of my hand and said I'll take care of that. He confided in me from time to time. He told about his wife who was slowing dying over the past 15 years of Multiple Sclerosis. He wouldn't let anyone else take care of her. He proudly showed me pictures of his daughter in the military. He loved beagles.

He still didn't look at me as he growled indignantly….

Isn't that something? Around here I can't get any of them to play ball. Work as a team.

They squabble, whine about every GD little thing and back- stab-each all day. Complaining about their shift assignments, crying about their problems with co-workers and inmates up on the floor. The stupid bastards locked up in here have the real problems. But you'd think those who have a good job just sitting around supervising the adult day care would have a little perspective on things. I swear to god sometimes I think they expect me to follow them into the Can and wipe their GD asses for them.

I've got a staff of men under me that a flock of Geese put to shame….

And he clicked the mouse to restart the animation.

And as I stood there looking at him, not knowing what to say next or even if that was a good idea.

Out of the profile corner of his eye one liquid crystal diamond appeared.

1/2010

Someone Else's Police Reports

There are voices carrying from the other room
However, there is no one there in person.
You understand.
A sort of interrogation
is in progress.
Alibis abound.
The sink is getting dripped on.
The clocks are getting ticked on.
Outside the sidewalks are getting stepped on.
The neighbors are watching for crime.
They haven't filed a report on you
yet this morning.

And there is nothing to be done with all this.
The lock downstairs is distinctive.
We know the sound of the key turning tumblers in autumn.
We know the sound of the door being jimmied in the Spring.
The cupboard doors of the kitchen are alive with dirty fingerprints.
Immediate family members and recent guests are all kept on file.

You would be advised to understand this.
After all, you could wind up being charged
With attempted armed robbery for trying to hold
Up the local Yellow Goose for $227.37
(Just after morning rush)
And then you'd get it.
You'll get stepped on.
The sink will get dripped on.
The clock will get ticked on.

Does all this give you a hard-on?
(well...not anymore)

So let the disorderly conduct commence.
Parking lot performances at the KWIK Fill
Seven Eleven Metro Jiffy Mart Winn Dixie Shop-N-Stop Gas It and
    Go
and of course the shit that just happens.

You'll be charged with something.
Trespassing here for a start. (Present or not)

This then became your aggravated vehicle
You operate erratic
Lost in emotional traffic.

2001

Nothing to See Here

-Well I honestly didn't think I was doing anything wrong. In the past there was always somebody to pay for what I wanted behind me.

-Actress Gene Tierney's explanation when caught shoplifting while
staring in the film Whirlpool (B & W 1947)

No Yellow crime scene tape.
No chalk outline of a victim on the asphalt.
A crowd didn't gather.
Perhaps someone wandered by on the way to
the store and might have glanced here
in this direction looking for something else.
Just curious.
That's all.
But really?
No one saw anything.
A bored cop took the complaint
from an anonymous source.
Turned out to be a false report anyway.
It was ascertained that truth was the only injured party.
But nobody could locate that
And it never showed up at the hearing anyway.
The only charges filed were dropped later
due to lack of any real evidence
Or indication of criminal intent.

So Enough.
Nothing to be seen here.
Not even Poetry was called in to question.
So just....
Move along.
Nothing to see here.

5/2011

Booking

A disembodied voice on the radio barks,
"INCOMING"
There is a "walk-in" waiting in the visiting lobby
For pictures and prints.
Did you bring your appearance ticket?

"How long is it going to be?"
"No, I don't know how long it's going to be"

Better make yourself comfortable.
Now lean down from the waist
And grab your ankles with your hands.

The snap of rubber gloves
Without either the benefit of
foreplay or an apology.

Just a job to be done here.
It isn't my fault that your ass
is bent over in front of me
reading like my job description.

I give up.
How deep do you want to go with this?
There are no easy topics in here
Small talk to make….
Tears won't help anything
Remorse is no longer an option.

You've been caught in the system.
No. Not my system.

You can contend it's not yours either.
But guess what?
I'm glad that I'm on my end.

How are things on your end?

Get dressed.
Officer will be with you as soon as he gets around to it.
You get one phone call.
Better start thinking about it now.
How long is it going to be?

No. I don't know how long it's going to be.

11/02

Summer
2/6/1996 – 6/30/2011

This sentence began
14 years ago on a bitter February night.
One snowy fringed bastard.
I was remained here from a factory floor
To the County facilities Sally-Port door.
Interned to teach.
Myself a lesson
and I had never been in jail before.

Now as this stolen Summer
mocks me the calendars bars swing in release
my period of incarceration comes to an end.

Time served.

Debt paid
In full......on the way out
with a white hot iron spade

I have endured incarceration
for my crimes of the heart.

Today I will walk
for the last time
down the sterile corridors
of the Ministry of Truth.
The Ministry of Love.
As the surveillance cameras
Overhead
Record every step in my exit.

I have been taught the lessons
of Room 101
and it was the worst thing in world.

Where of course
I confessed to everything.
Implicated everyone.
Betrayed one and all.
Including this
As she said,
"I did what I had to do"

So I told them,

"To do it to you too."

That was expected.
That was the provisional condition
for contemplation of charges
not being dropped
but instead
burned into my flesh indelibility.

In return
The shackles are coming off today.
I will clean out my cell.
My classroom
and box my few possessions.
Surrender my keys to the proper authorities
Take off my identification badge.
Leaving my fellow inmates
Their GEDs
a modest decent library I help build
in silence to better
To contemplate

The weight of
their own crimes.

The bars will split open today
and I will emerge for the last time
from the basement classroom
to the elevator that takes forever
to go up or down
But spends most its' time in here
Going….. somehow
Sideways in recidivism.

Time now to plea bargain
the three lock down gates
and out into the parking lot of
blinding light and smoldering asphalt
sizzling in dizzying heat
of this Summer stolen.

Still guilty
Not forgiven anything
but still being watched.
No rehabilitation
Remorse in only
all the those years coming this.

Time served
in this sentence with you.

Released contingent on this condition
I would be
remanded to remember
everything.

The time surrendered in here

ending with one last final mark of stigmata justice.
I was to be branded with a scalding cattle iron
that was embossed into my flesh
and left an pronounced abrasion
into the shape of the letter D
as indelible as my birthmarks
to define the flesh they call me.

And I will only shed these scarlet scars
upon discarding my flesh letters into eternity.
But.
For now
That sentence.
This sentence.
My sentence
is over.

6-30-2011

Lucky, Lulu, and a Cat Named Bo

(Cold Turkey)

Sixth floor walkup in an old tenement building
next to the Ukie funeral parlor on 7th Street.
Thanksgiving, 3:00pm.
Black and white TV on,
rabbit ears up, sound off.

Thanksgiving Day Parade is over.
Santa's been safely delivered to Macys,
to the delight of children everywhere.
Nothin' on but football
for the rest of the day.

Lulu's passed out drunk and naked
in the old clawfoot bathtub.
Bo's curled up on her belly
purring and kneading her chest with his paws,
as if trying to revive her with the power of his love.
She's holdin' onto an empty pint of Svedka.
Looks like our planned Thanksgiving dinner
ain't gonna' happen.

I turn off the bathroom light,
put on my peacoat and Mets cap,
and split,
leaping down the narrow spiral staircase
two steps at a time,
still tryin' to trick my body
into thinkin' it's three floors instead of six.

I hit the sidewalk and head toward 2nd Avenue,
turning up my collar and tipping my head down
to block the damp wind.
I stop at Big Bar
but it's closed for the holiday.
Circle back toward 1st to Blue and Gold,
It's closed too.
Walk up to Tile Bar on the corner,
Damn…. closed.
I cross 1st, pick up a pack of rolling papers
at the bodega,
then check International Bar next door.
CLOSED sign in the window.

It's grey, windy, and desolate.
No traffic; no people.
Cold, sad, and frustrated,
headin' South on 1st Ave,
I'm thinkin' I'll probably end up
at McDonald's with a freakin' "Happy Meal"
and nothin' to drink.
Just about to go in Mickey D's
when I notice lights on
in the window of Coal Yard Bar
next door.
It's open. *Fuck yeah!*

I step in to find the joint full of locals,
who like me,
are lookin' for some solace and sanctuary
on a lonely holiday.
I grab the only remaining seat
on the far curve of the horseshoe bar,
hang my coat on the back of the stool,
and settle in for a look around;

spottin' Blondie and Boho,
Gator, Roadrunner, Snake,
and the usual coyotes
from the local bars.

Across from the bar, the wall is lined with tables
filled with foil baking trays of turkey, mashed potatoes,
stuffing, string beans, and cranberry sauce.
There are stacks of paper plates, napkins, and plastic utensils.
Folks are helping themselves to this holiday feast
offered free to anyone who wanders in.

We're breakin' bread with family today,
defined for us by circumstance or misfortune,
but family it is:
All the social misfits and outcasts
who've chosen dive bars as their comfort zone.

From across the bar,
my writer friend Blondie waves and smiles a big hello
as I'm makin' my way to the food tables.
I offer only a mechanical nod and my best fake smile.
I fill a plate high with stuffing, douse it with gravy,
and return to my stool,
to wash it down with C.C. and soda.

An attractive young lady sashays up
and asks in a thick Liverpool accent,
if I'd mind "chatting" with her for a bit.
I'm feelin' pretty low
and don't even wanna' talk to my bar buds.
I don't sense any kind of "hittin' on me" vibe,
so I ask her what's up with her.
She says she's from Ibiza,
freelances for Vogue magazine Europe

doing lifestyle stories,
and is here to do a story on dive bars.
(What the fuck??? Is she for real?)

Tells me my tatts are cool,
thinks I've been around a lot,
and might be interesting to interview.
I reluctantly agree,
but only if she'll spring for a drink.
She does.
I order a double Makers
instead of my usual cheap shit.

She asks a bunch of rudely inquisitive, insulting,
and demeaning questions
about me and the type of people who hang in dive bars.
I'm embarrassed and pissed-off
so I reply with subtly sarcastic answers
that go right over her empty head.
I think they'll probably satisfy the preconceived notions
of her faux aristocrat readers,
who they think know who we are, and what we do.
It's total bullshit and she eats it up,
'cause it's what she wants to hear.
I'm done, and she moves on,
after I hit her up for another double Maker's.

Brenda, the bartender asks what's up with the chick.
When I tell her the bogus answers I gave to her asshole questions,
she laughs sayin', "Just a *Euro-trash vampire*
lookin' to taste some wild coyote blood."
She "high-fives" me and pours another double Makers,
on the house.

I finish up my stuffing,
with a C.C. and soda for the road,
and fill up a big take-home plate
of cold turkey scraps and spuds,
sloshed with lots of thick cold gravy.
I know Lulu's gonna' be hungry
when she wakes up.
I leave with a quick nod toward my friends.

Blondie follows me out.
"Hey.... Lucky.... You're actin' like a real shit.
What the fuck's goin' on?"
"Yeah, sorry. I'm just in a dark holiday hole right now.
. . . . You know. . . . I'll be alright. . . . See ya'."
"Lulu off her meds again?"
I shake my head, "Yeah."
"Wow, sorry!" kisses me on the cheek,
and she's gone.

Feelin' a little woozy.
Just go through the motions and get outta' here:
Lift collar,
pull down brim,
hands in pockets,
slow easy steps,
and ……. I'm gone with the wind.

Lulu's up and in the bathroom brushin' her teeth
when I finally get back.
I lean in and notice a mean lookin' black and blue on her hip,
from fallin' in the bathtub, I guess.
Don't see any blood or open wounds
so I think we're good.
Bo's sittin' up on the toilet tank
watchin' Lulu brush.

I roll a doobie and we smoke at the kitchen table,
laughing as she wolfs down the cold take-home
and tosses turkey scraps down to Bo,
who pounces on them with delight.
Nodding her head repeatedly in satisfaction,
she looks up and smiles.

Buzzed from the bar and pretty stoned,
I'm mesmerized by her naked body.
She looks beautiful,
even under the stark bare kitchen bulb.
Thinkin' I might just get lucky tonight
if she don't start drinkin' again too soon.

I know we don't look like your Norman Rockwell
Thanksgiving Family portrait,
but we're all we've got, and it'll have to do.

-Phillip Giambri aka the Ancient Mariner 6/2018

The Alcoholic Cycle

For Odis

I really can't recall seeing him come in the bar and seat himself down in the far end. The light that time of day from the street in late June afternoon washed in glaring bright and white hot brilliance flooding the barroom with blind spots and shadow corners.

Early in your shift there is always plenty of prep to do-clean out the sinks, refill with fresh tabs of sanitizer, slice up the lemons and limes, check the beer coolers for restock (if it wasn't done the night before.) It was all part of the routine of waking the bar up for another night.

The doors had been open for about half an hour and so far the bar had been empty until this guy appeared bereft of the usual early bird regulars who showed up after work. It was like he had been conjured out of thin air on the barstool. He looked like a pale silent ghost almost ethereal in general appearance. I guessed he was somewhere in his fifties. It was difficult to know almost like there wasn't enough physical evidence for me to judge and at that time anybody who was over twenty five I regarded as old.

So when I regarded this first customer of my shift I saw a pale slight fragile looking gentleman with sparse salt and pepper beard, thinning widows' peak crown. He was wearing a worn blue Terry cloth wrap around his mid-section, a newly laundered white V-neck Tee-Shirt and flip-flops.

He never did acknowledge me or call me over to serve him. He was staring ahead at some unknown point of focus as he gingerly with shaking hands lit a Salem Menthol and exhaled a bluish plume of smoke as if to announce his presence. I came down to where he was sitting wiping my hands on the bar towel and asked as friendly as possible; *Hey... How you doing sir and what can I do for you?*

It seemed to barely register for a moment and then he seemed to return from whatever space he had been lost in while his bird like shoulders shuddered then sank and rasped out in barely audible voice just above a whisper; *I'd like a draft beer please.* Sure thing I said *What kind?*. Looking down at the bar top avoiding eye contact I heard him say *Does it really matter?*

Well it sure didn't matter to me-little strange I thought and pulled the Tap closest to right hand and filled him a Mug of Old Milwaukie (we sold a lot of that in those days) and sat it down before him. He eyeballed it for a one-thousand to ten count and then with a really shaky grasp raised to his lips spilling some of head and drank off three quarters in one gulp and did a pronounced wince. Dam I thought- maybe I showed have cleaned out those taps. I asked; *Hey Mister is the beer ok?* Again with no eye contact mumbled; *sure it's fine.* I tried a little bar humor- *Guess that first one goes down kinda rough huh?* He didn't laugh.

At once I realized I was probably staring at him a bit too long and intently trying figure out just what the deal was with this stranger here. Besides I needed to get back to work, seeing that the usual bar banter was unlikely forth coming and the Happy Hour rush was due in any minute like the tide from the bay across the street on the waterfront wharfs.

But-no. Over the course of the next hour it stayed pretty quiet. A few regulars and stray tourists looking for a couple of quick cold ones and shot before suppertime. Over the course of this time my first customer worked through three drafts in rapid succession- each one disappearing faster than one that preceded it. They were going down smoother and faster now, Seemed like every time I looked up his glass was empty-but he never gestured to me for another one. But I did ask the next time- *refill Mister?* This time he looked me straight in the eye and with some vibrancy in a stronger direct voice replied- *Yea- just keep them coming and I'd like a shot of Dewar's Scotch straight up- no ice- in fact can you make that double?*

I poured the shots into a glass and set it down on the bar. This time about 2 seconds after leaving my hand? It was gone. One gulp. No wince this time. In fact now he actually smiled with a profound air of satisfaction and said to me- *Ok now young man-what's your name?* Of the ensuing conversation(if you could call it that) I don't have much to report now or even back then. I was a college dropout back in my hometown for the Summer and perhaps foreseeable future with very little clue about what came next(if anything).

This was the first time I had ever held a job as a bartender and was still pretty green at it. Only reason I had this gig at all was because the owner was an old friend from my not so distant teenage years who was looking out for me. I wasn't very good at, hardly looked the part either in appearance or years and the other owners daughter hated my guys-hated having to work with me and would keep her distance with a clear distain when she came in later at ten.

Meanwhile now this guy (I don't think he ever gave his name) had developed a real personality and evidently decided we were old friends. Gone was the barely there ghost of a few hours ago. He was full of advice for me and observations on life. And now he was putting the booze away at a rapid pace- drinking the double Dewar's in tall water glasses on the rocks.

From what I could gather he was some sort of artist or something he was speaking rather now with some authority about philosophers- their philosophy; classical music composers of the Renaissance, specific movements of painters and their work, lots of reference to writers and poetry. Some names I might have barely recognized for my rather brief failed time in college. But really it was all over my head and coming so fast and disjointed I could barely keep up. By the way? Just for the record? He had started to laugh at his own jokes vigorously.

And now he was mapping out my future for me. I should travel. Go to Europe-study ancient civilizations- books I needed to read-music I should listen to-Art I needed to appreciate. Next thing I know he's shifting gears advising me to become a plumber or electrician instead.

Well- this was all well and good- He seemed like just another regular now who sounded like he had just come to from his dark funk. He was clearly digging the attention being my Humanities teacher only problem was the bar was starting to get really busy now. I had to hustle to keep up tending to the influx of the crowd. The sun was setting and the crowd washed in riding the tide.
High and dry.

Soon the light from the front window gave way to the barroom lights. Most of the stools were full now and the jukebox was blaring while laughter and loud conversations filled the room. Remember now he was all the way down the other end of the bar. I couldn't get down there fast enough to keep up with him, much less listen to his pontifications.

Trouble was I couldn't be his captive audience anymore.
And that's when the trouble started.

Then the guy decided that he had been waiting too long for his next drink. He slammed his glass down on the bar top with such force that it shattered into shards spraying glass and liquid all over the place. Naturally most of heads closest to him swung in his direction. Well now he had his audience. I don't remember how long his rant went- but it was loud and obscenity laden cryptic rage. The immediate effect was people were laughing and shaking their heads. Instead of appearing menacing or profound he had become comical.

And then all at once he just shut down. Fell silent. Of course I went down to his spot to clean up the mess, wipe the counter of the broken glass, ice and spilled booze. I tried to apologize for not getting to him sooner-set him up with another round telling him it was on the house. He never said a word-in fact? He wouldn't even look at me.

The next hour was a blur. Costumers were stacked up three deep at the bar waiting to order. By ten o'clock when the other bartender (who hated me) came on shift the place was swinging in a raucous, rowdy din. As fate would have it the guy was down sitting on her end of the bar. She was going to have to deal with him now. I clearly recall her shooting me a venomous glare suggesting *–you made this mess and I'm going to have to clean it up.*

I noticed that he was still going at his two fisted soak, but the pace has slowed down. The other bartender had seen to that. He had his head down now and appeared to be mumbling quietly to himself. One more observation in foreshadowing. He had started to wobble. The last time he went to the Can he did figure 8s and had to hold on to whatever was handy to steady himself.

Around one thirty in the morning there was very loud bang down the end of the bar. In was obvious somebody had just hit the deck and hard. Of course it was his spot that was empty. He was out cold on the barroom floor with his barstool on its side next him.

Well- now what? A regular and me couldn't get him to come to. We stood over him shaking our heads. The majority of the patrons were ignoring the whole scene. The other bartender disappeared down my end of the bar, as if to say – *nice work dipshit- I hope this gets you fired.*

Just then my friend, the owner came in the back door – stood there with his hands on his hips, shaking his head. Without a word to anybody, he just picked the guy up, carried him towards the front door and out into the street- depositing him gently on the curb next to a parking meter. He walked back in with a deep poker face and it was business to usual until closing time. Soon it was just him and I shooing the last barflies out for the night.

I looked out in the street. The guy had not yet moved from where he was in the gutter. As the last lights were extinguished I just stood there still looking and then there was a hand on my shoulder. My old friend asked what I thought had happened tonight. I started to explain as best I could but the owner stopped me mid-sentence. He said rather sadly and kindly *I'll tell you exactly happened-*

That guy came in early hours ago looking like death warmed over. After a few beers he woke up and for about a hour, with more beers and shots seemed like anybody else. Then at some point after drink after drink he got loud and went ballistic and further down the road just passed out cold- do you know what that's called?

I shook my head.

That my young friend is called the Alcoholic Cycle- 3 drinks to get going 4-7 drinks to fuel the fire. 8-12 to fully detonate. Beyond that the blackout curtain fell and he passed out cold. I've dealt with this guy before-with slight variations it's always the same. In the future you've got to recognize this with customers and back off- slowing them down or cut it off all together. Don't worry I'll always back you up on this. It's your duty and call as a bartender. Do you understand what I'm saying here?

I nodded. Then looked back out the door to guy on the curb next to a parking meter and asked, *is he going to be ok?*

Owner just shrugged with both palms up- *sure I guess- maybe- probably. He'll come to around first light in a few hours and lurch home or the cops might pick him up and give him a place to sleep it off.*

And tomorrow? He'll do the whole thing over again- not in here, but somewhere –but I want you remember what you saw tonight.

I had to ask- *Do you know his name?*

Once again the owner with the sad smile- *Young man when you ride the Alcoholic Cycle?*

-You don't have a name anymore,

June 2018

Lightning Source UK Ltd.
Milton Keynes UK
UKHW04n0151280718
326420UK00002B/4/P